a story

that

matters

a story
that
matters

a gratifying
approach to
writing about
your life

by

GINA L. CARROLL

Published by SparkPress, a BookSparks imprint,
A division of SparkPoint Studio, LLC
Tempe, Arizona, USA, 85281
www.gosparkpress.com

Published 2017
Printed in the United States of America
ISBN: 978-1-943006-12-0 (pbk)
ISBN: 978-1-943006-13-7 (e-bk)

Library of Congress Control Number: 2017932266

Cover design © Julie Metz, Ltd./metzdesign.com
Book design by Stacey Aaronson

*Permission to use Lois Daniel's concept of ground rules granted by
Chicago Review Press.*

*Names and identifying characteristics have been changed to protect the privacy of
certain individuals.*

CONTENTS

INTRODUCTION

Everybody loves a good story. We like to connect with others by recognizing what is familiar and similar between us. We like to be shocked and awed by what is different and unique. We want to know the history of how people became who they are. We also love to live vicariously through them, enjoying the opportunity to step into the shoes of both acquaintances and strangers, even if only momentarily. Our brains are adept at extracting meaning and learning lessons from stories. We naturally think in story form.

As a blogger, storytelling is my stock and trade. Bloggers often use our own stories to connect our readers not only to ourselves, but also to certain issues, causes, products, and services. Storytelling, for bloggers, is a more personal approach to information sharing; it is an utter embrace of the recognition that human beings have as much of an affinity to stories as we do to sugar. Similar to the urgings of our natural sweet tooth, we are drawn practically from birth to stories, even before we consciously choose them.

Celebrated American author John Edgar Wideman says that people like stories:

> Because they're like maps. We use a story as a kind of piece of information to orient ourselves, make sense of the loneliness, make sense of what we'll never be able to decipher: the enigma that surrounds us.[1]

---

1 Kathryn Shattuck, "All Around Town, Stories Well Told," The *New York Times*, March 3, 2011, available online at: http://www.nytimes.com/2011/03/04/arts/04readings.html?_r=1.

Scientists have long been fascinated by our natural predilection for stories. Our brains are somehow wired to love and to be drawn to tales, real and fictional. And because of this, as Adam Gopnik of the *New Yorker* says, stories are the currency of life.

Across the industries of our world, stories reign supreme. In the best films, the story is more important than the stars and the fanfare. In business, the story is the core of all marketing. From the Fortune 500 company, all the way down to the individual job seeker, our employers, customers, and colleagues want to know our story; our professional success often depends on how well we tell it.

This book is a road map to writing your life stories. In it, you will find a dogged devotion to the philosophy that every life story is really a combination of many stories. And these stories matter. They are important enough to put down in writing, and to share. To assist you in your efforts to write your stories, I offer an approach that my writing-services business partner, Carol, and I use in our *Tell Your Story* workshops. In these workshops, we explore ways of telling stories from five seminal periods of a lifetime: the story of your mother, your childhood, your love stories, your professional journey, and your spiritual awakening. Complete with prompts and examples, the chapters that follow are designed to inspire, motivate, and challenge you. They will help you write the stories that matter to you.

In recent years, plenty of memoirs have been written and published, and many more are on the way. In fact, the memoir genre continues to flourish. In 2010, Daniel Mendelsohn, in the *New Yorker,* called the rise in published memoirs not

just a flood, but a tsunami. Since then the numbers and demand for the true stories of others have only risen. Does the
availability of so many life stories diminish the importance of
yours? The answer is an emphatic no. In a very real sense—in
ways that I will explore later in this book—the inclusion of
your voice and your story is all the more important. And so,
we endeavor to jump into the mix here. Knowing that we
love a good story, we shall set out to tell our own. We will
answer the call of the insatiable human hunger for a story.
And by telling our own stories, we plug ourselves into the
human continuum of time, of history, and of pleasure.

CHAPTER ONE

Why Your Stories Matter

hy is your story so important? Why is the writing of your life story such a big deal that others—certainly the author of this book—feel compelled to encourage you in that direction? There are many excellent reasons to get our stories down in written form. Once you get past the feeling that your story will not be interesting (it will), then you must embrace the fact that you are an important part of history—at least someone's history. You have played a starring role in the lives of your spouse or lover, your children, your friends, and your colleagues, including your current workmates and the professional people coming behind you. These are the folks who have a vested interest in your life experiences and how you came to be who you are now. In addition, there are people whom you may never know or meet that can be profoundly affected by your words. When you write and put your story out into the universe of story lovers—and we have already established that this group pretty much includes the entire human race—you may set in motion your own Butterfly Effect, wherein the small ripple of your story, like the flap of a single butterfly wing, may cause the proverbial hurricane on the other side of the world. That ripple-turned-hurricane has the potential power to provide help, hope, and connection for someone in need.

However, the most powerful benefits might happen internally for you. The exercise of writing your own life stories is a journey and a gift that you give yourself. It is a rewarding endeavor that allows time for reflection and revelation. In more ways than I can predict for you right now, you may very well be the greatest beneficiary of your writing. And that, my new friend, is reason enough.

YOUR HISTORY IS YOUR FAMILY'S HISTORY

"Anyone who's fortunate enough to live to be fifty years old should take some time, even if it's just a couple of weekends, to sit down and write the story of your life, even if it's only twenty pages, and even if it's only for your children and grandchildren."

—Former President Bill Clinton[2]

---

2 President Clinton's advice, arguably (though perhaps inadvertently), also makes the case for beginning to write your life stories before you reach your fiftieth birthday. Why wait? Any age is a good time to begin recording your stories. And the closer the writing to the actual occurrence, the more accurate the account.

What Ken Dychtwald, "Age Wave" expert and best-selling author of sixteen books on aging-related issues, has to say about the importance of family history may surprise you:

Many people wrongly assume that the most important issue among families is money and wealth transfer— it's not. What we found was the memories, the stories, the values were ten times more important to people than the money.[3]

This only becomes more apparent as we age, and like all works of art, our written story becomes even more priceless once we are gone. Recently, my family placed my grandmother in a memory-care facility. She has Alzheimer's. In her prime and until very recently, she was a very mentally sharp, astute, and engaged woman. She was a proud finder and keeper of facts. And so the person she is now feels quite foreign to us, and we are already grieving the loss of an enormous part of her: her memory. As my mother packed up my grandmother's bedroom, she came across a little bag of old letters. They turned out to be letters that my great-grandfather and great-grandmother exchanged before they were married in the 1920s, after he moved from Birmingham, Alabama to Chicago for work. He was a part of the great African-American migration from the South to the North.

These letters contain both a personal account of this interesting time in American history *and* a love story that is the

---

3 American Legacies Study, Allianz Life Insurance Company of North America.

genesis of my grandmother's life. My mother's discovery of these letters was a bittersweet emotional moment. She lamented my grandmother's inability to discuss the letters and the history surrounding them, since my grandmother is the only person still living who could have filled in the details of this story. Yet, my mother was thrilled to find these written accounts that, with my grandmother's loss of memory, would have also been forever lost to the rest of us.

This family discovery happened just as I began writing this book, and it serves as a perfect illustration of American writer Richard Louv's statement:

> *"Our stories, our personal stories, our family stories, are our real gold. If we're lucky, as we age, we put our stories in the bank, where they gather interest in deepening meaning."*

The truth is, our stories are not just *our* stories. Our life stories are part of the many bundles that make up the life stories of our family members and everyone else we have touched along the way.

Daniel Taylor said in his book, *The Healing Power of Stories*, that "Families are united more by mutual stories—of love and pain and adventure—than by biology." We should not underestimate the power our stories have to connect, to inform, and to help our families. When a person visits a doctor in pursuit of a physical, the doctor will inquire about his or her medical history; a crucial part of that person's history will be the medical history of his or her parents. Your genetic makeup and your related medical predispositions—challenges and advantages you pass or do not pass on to your children—will most assuredly have an impact on their health. This reality is also true beyond the medical context, in every other aspect of your life.

I will explore this truth further in the upcoming chapter, "My Mother's Lessons," because who your mother is, whether she raised you or not, has influenced who you are. Similarly, you—and the stories you tell—affect who your children are and who they will become. And so, your early stories are important to your children and will be increasingly so, even if this is not so apparent right now.

Your stories are important even if they don't include fairy-tale happy endings or glowing testimonials of familial perfection. Some stories may be painful, hurtful, or difficult to reveal. Their telling and the resultant impact on others might be distressing, but the stories' imperfections do not in any way diminish their importance or their potential to help and heal.

Many of your stories may already be well known by your family members. In fact, chances are that some of your stories are legends in their own right! But I want, here, to draw a distinction between telling your story and putting it in writing. If your story or stories are not written, they are at risk of being forgotten, or more likely, changed. Though we may value the way oral stories evolve into wholly different stories over time, if you want to maintain the integrity of *your* story, and if it is important for you to establish and maintain the truth (or at least your version of it), than your best bet is to put it in print, once and for all. Like my great-grandparents' letters, our stories have the potential to long outlive us. If you value the preservation of your stories, then they are much safer in print.

Your Story Is Your Own

✦

"You must have control of the authorship of your own destiny. The pen that writes your life story must be held in your own hand."

—Irene C. Kassorla

The popularity of Kathryn Stockett's book, *The Help*, illustrates the importance of telling our own stories. This engaging fictional account of one woman's quest to forge a writing career in the South during the civil rights era centers, in large part, on African-American domestic workers of that time. The main character, who is not African-American, resembles the author in many ways, as the author has drawn from her own early years in Jackson, Mississippi. However, since the story's real focus is the African-American characters of whom she has only provided enough of a sketch to move the story along, you can't help but hunger for more depth and authenticity for these characters. The stories of African-American domestic workers in pre–civil rights America are rich, diverse, and complicated tales that deserve to be told with their true complexity and fullness of humanity. All writers have a right to share their version of an era, especially in fiction. But as we experience the real stories from people of a certain time period, like the civil rights era, we will be less likely to settle for portrayals that diminish their experiences or gloss over the adversity they overcame at such an important historical turning point.

There are stories in print about the civil rights era that

are penned by African-American women, and yet, the widespread promotion and popularity of the highly stylized version offered in *The Help* says something about the need for more. Many African-American women bought and read the book and viewed the movie version, connecting to the parts that rang true for them, their mothers and grandmothers. There ought to be more stories that are truer and more authentic for the women who crave them.

We must share our own stories and make them available for those who would use them for historical and artistic purposes. We owe this to the world and to ourselves. Viola Davis, who was nominated for a best actress Oscar in a leading role for her portrayal of Aibileen Clark in the movie version of *The Help*, had this to say about the importance of storytelling in her now-famous speech at the 2012 Women in Hollywood event:

What keeps me in the business is hope, and that's the hope that women of color are also a part of the narrative, that our stories are just as potent, because we also have the power of transformation. We also have the power to be quirky, and sexy, and different, funny, heartfelt—all of those things. And I consider it to be a larger purpose in life that keeps me in the business. My mother has an eighth-grade education, and she started having children and got married at fifteen. Her mother got married at fifteen and had babies at fifteen. Eighteen children she had. My mom had six. And she grew up, she had all of her children at home in my grandmother's house. My grandmother

gave birth to all of us. And I happen to think that my
mom's story is very interesting. Very interesting. And
those are the stories I want to see on screen just as
much as anybody else's story. . . . And I believe and I
really hope that we have the imagination, that we
have the courage to bring those stories to life, because
I want to do . . . what Cicely Tyson did to me . . . she
allowed me to have the visual of what it means to
dream. When I saw her in The Autobiography of Miss
Jane Pittman, she threw me a rope. . . .[4]

There are so many ways that you, as the writer of your own story, can throw others a rope. Your story can allow another person to reflect on a time, a way of being, an emotion, or a viewpoint. And that illumination or reflection can be life changing in ways that are predictable and not so predictable. And yet, the uniqueness of your own individual telling makes it a solitary stance with which you stake your place in the world.

So, the importance of this effort to get your stories written goes beyond the notion of storytelling. Just as important to the collective consciousness is the imperative that you be the master of the telling and the writing of the stories that are yours and yours alone.

---

4 Women in Hollywood 2012, AOL.com, available online at
http://on.aol.com/video/viola-davis-women-in-hollywood-speech-517183460.

To Help Others

"We only have what we give."
—Isabel Allende

Recently I wrote a story about my grandmother and how I believe her love of sweets (and her consumption of sugar) eventually contributed to her death. The main point of the story was that I, myself, have a profound sweet tooth, as she did, and I fear that my consumption of sweets will be my undoing as well. Weeks after that story was published, in the midst of a business meeting, one of the other meeting participants pulled out a copy of my article and said that it had completely described her relationship with sweets and piqued her consciousness about the dangers of her diet. My article was her call to action, the sign and the catalyst to make an important change in her life. I am often amazed by and impressed with how unique, personal accounts—writings extremely specific to the writer—can so profoundly affect others.

Cancer bloggers—men, women, and even children who write about their own or a loved one's cancer battle—take to the Internet in large numbers to chronicle their experiences. Many of them have large and loyal followings because their stories connect them to other sufferers. These connections are important for everyone involved. Dennis Pyritz of the Being Cancer Network [of bloggers] says this about the importance of the written experiences for cancer victims and survivors:

There are lessons to be learned from every story of cancer, lessons to be learned from every stage and phase of our struggles. In fact, that is our reason for publishing guest posts in the first place. Some lessons are dearer than others to learn. Some posts are harder than others to read. . . . One could argue that there is nothing noble in suffering, that there is little to admire in death. And yet that is part of the transcendent nature of human experience—that meaning can be derived from both.[5]

You can help people in small and enormous ways with your story. But two things are required for your impact to be felt: one, that you get your story written, and two, that you share it.

The religious and spiritual among us already know this about the power of testimony. A testimony is composed of what one has learned along life's journey and how God manifests in one's life. The tradition of sharing testimonies is a long and important one in many religions and spiritual disciplines. What is the *Bible* but a collection of spiritual stories of people's encounters with God that teach and guide believers?

The *Bible* also encourages the sharing of testimonies. Believers are directed to bear witness to God's works in their lives and on their behalf. Mark, in chapter 5, verse 19, says:

---

5 See http://www.beingcancer.net for more information.

And he did not permit him but said to him, "Go home to your friends and tell them how much the Lord has done for you, and how he has had mercy on you."

In John 15:27, Jesus directs his disciples:

And you also will bear witness, because you have been with me from the beginning.

Indeed, the many spiritual lessons one attains become even more valuable in proportion to the extent that they are shared with others. This is a large part of our spiritual obligation. Many believe that the act of testimony is how one reaffirms his or her faith and connects with other believers.

It is no accident that Christian self-help is one of the fastest growing book genres, as it capitalizes on the crossroads in a life story where one encounters the spiritual, and the lessons learned from that crossing. Not only might your testimony be your most rewarding life story, but as a writer in the current market, your testimony may very well be your best way to break into publishing.

FOR YOURSELF

✦

"Ultimately, the richest resource for meaning and healing is one we already possess. It rests (mostly untapped) in the material of our own life story, in the sprawling, many-layered 'text' that has been accumulating within us across the years."

—Gary M. Kenyon and William L. Randall,
Restorying Our Lives: Personal Growth through Autobiographical Reflection

Lastly, but in no way least, write your own story for yourself. Just as testimony can help you clarify and solidify your religious and spiritual beliefs, your other life stories can help you put your experiences and their lessons into perspective. Writing your stories, articulating what you have done and seen and endured, what you have taught and learned and contributed, where you've made mistakes and failed, allow you to take stock and contemplate where you are going. Sue William Silverman in her book *Fearless Confessions: A Writer's Guide to Memoir* says:

Writing my life is a gift I give to myself. To write is to be constantly reborn. On one page, I understand this about myself. On the next page, I understand that.

If you are reading this book, chances are you are already compelled to write. I hope you are now motivated with the knowledge that your story is important to you, important to your family, and important to many others whom you may know or may never know. Your story is a part of something big, the fabric of history, and of the human experience. Once it is written and shared, your story will change *someone*. I guarantee it.

What Matters Most in Chapter One

1. Your life story is important to your family: your children and grandchildren. Your story is the beginning of their story.

2. You must be the teller of the stories that matter to you. Your experiences are threads in the fabric of human history. This is why they are best told by you.

3. Your stories can help others far beyond those you expect to reach.

4. Writing your life story helps you take stock of who you are, where you've been, and where you are going.

CHAPTER TWO

Story of a Girl, Story of a Boy: Writing About Your Childhood

"The childhood shows the man, as morning shows the day."
—John Milton, English poet

Our early years are called formative years for a reason. Most of us believe that we, as adults, are the sum total of all that happened in our childhoods, and that the beginning of our story is the very core of our life narrative. So when we consider the stories of our childhood, we tend to approach them with a certain reverence for all that they mean about and to us.

You may find that reveling in the stories of your childhood is a little like peering into the life of another. Who is that child—that girl or boy—you will be writing about? Who is that *you* that is not likely the same *you* that you are now? This reality is a point of interest. How exactly did you get from being that girl to this woman, that boy to this man? What are the seminal stories that happened in between?

As a child, I was painfully shy. Those of us who *used to be shy* rarely use the word "shy" without the adjective "painfully." Shyness, at least for me, was a kind of prison. I was a funny, theatrical, silly child, who was locked behind bars not so much of insecurity, as of an overly oppressive sense of propriety. For some reason, I was certain that outward displays of folly and social initiative were inappropriate and unwanted. And so, even at the urging of others, I would not (could not) speak out, even to say hello, in public. At home and around my closest relatives, however, I was a cut-up. I was a dancing, storytelling, joking, arguing, singing whirlwind of a child. But when my parents would share my antics with their friends, their friends would look at me, the little squirrelly girl hiding behind her mother, with expressions of doubt and justifiable disbelief. I am sure they thought my mother was a wishful-thinking mother in denial. When I encounter shy children now, it is with great empathy. I can also connect with frustrated adults who must deal with children brimming with potential and talent, but who are too shy to let it show.

My grandmother was one such frustrated adult. I once promised her that I would perform a song with my guitar for her church group. My grandmother was a bona fide church lady. She was one of the matrons of her church, greatly respected and deeply involved. She, after all, was director of the usher board! She'd heard me sing this particular song and play it many times at home when she finally exclaimed that it was time to share the lovely tune with others. I reluctantly relented to her loving insistence. When the fateful day came, I had every intention of singing and playing that well-practiced song. And, in fact, after a glowing introduction to the crowd by my grandmother, I did begin to play—one stanza, two stanzas . . . three—and still no words did I utter. I was shaking and breathless, so much so that when the time came to begin singing, I just could not make the words come out. I simply could not. And so . . . the church audience was treated to a lovely instrumental piece by Sister Avery's granddaughter—none the wiser that singing was also supposed to occur. My grandmother, of course, knew I had chickened out, but expressed pride that I had at least been able to get as far as I did.

That poor wordless girl. When did she "grow out" of her reservations and trepidations? Well, the road from shy girl to who I am now was a long and winding one, full of stories about risk, and big and small triumphs and failures. Those stories make up one of the many bountiful gardens of experiences from which I can pick and choose.

You do not need to contemplate this question—how did you get from there to here—in its totality when you are writing the stories of your youth. All you have to do is start writing one story at a time as they come up in your memory. As your stories come together, the from-here-to-there question will likely answer itself. If you have already chosen to start your life story with your childhood, you likely have a story or two that are important to you or that you feel are meaningful to tell. And that is enough for a beginning.

If a story has not bubbled up for you yet, perhaps Graham Greene can help. Greene was a British author credited with the wise observation: "There is always one moment in child-hood when the door opens and lets the future in." The door opened for me and allowed me to escape my prison of shyness when my mother signed me up to be a cheerleader for my brother's Pop Warner football team. She signed me on without my knowing; I would have never agreed. She bought the cute uniform and the awesome matching socks and bows. And with a group of other shy new recruits, I learned to yell loudly and shake my *groove-thang* in public. In my mother's brilliance, she found the perfect coming out. In me, a career cheerleader was born. Despite the intensely competitive and highly controversial nature of cheerleading these days, I think of cheerleading as my liberation, which is probably why I continued to cheer and dance before rowdy sports fans from elementary school all the way through college.

Greene's quote so aptly captures this and all of those crucial turning points in childhood when things change or shift, where learning accelerates or meaning envelops us and we are moved forward in a new and transformative way. When were those moments for you? They do not need to be earth-shattering to create a significant shift. Find one of those, perhaps the earliest you can think of, and write down the moment as a prompt for yourself. Next, begin to describe the circumstances surrounding or leading up to that moment.

There are many, many ways to start a story. This idea of a turning point is just one. I have included additional prompts for your childhood story in Chapter Seven. Beginning can be a challenge unless you remember that the most important act is to start—to put pen to paper, fingertips to keyboard. You may revise your beginning once you have your first draft written. So let's pave the way for a strong start, smooth middle, and fantastic finish.

TAKE COMFORT, WRITING IS HARD

I want to state right up front the admission that writing is hard, because too often, beginners have a notion that writing, especially writing about your own experiences, should come easily. And when the novice has a difficult time beginning or runs into a block, she might conclude that she is not cut out to be a real writer. For some, this is enough to halt their progress or even terminate their effort altogether. So you should know that the challenges you may face as you work at getting your story down are not unique to you and do not disqualify you as worthy to write.

Any professional writer can tell you that telling a story well is a process, and that process is not always linear. It will require sorting through your memories and finagling your words to craft a narrative that is complete, truthful, and compelling. This process can sometimes be complicated and frustrating as you struggle to decide what to include. Sometimes, deciding what *not* to include is an even greater challenge. I discuss the challenge of deciding what to include in Chapter Three.

The discouragement I encountered early in my writing career halted my writing altogether for several years. When I decided that I wanted to write, I thought it wise to begin by journaling. After sitting at my desk hovering over those empty pages for many days, I concluded that if I could not even get my own personal thoughts into a private journal, how was I ever going to be a writer? I pushed my chair away from my desk, never to return to the journal. Fortunately, this was not the end of my writing story. A friend invited me to a book-signing event, the *Houston Chronicle* Book and Author Dinner. This annual event features both new and established authors who have recently published. The featured authors are given the opportunity to speak.

Jonathan Harr was one of the authors to speak on this particular evening. His book, *A Civil Action*, had just been published and was receiving great reviews. But according to his speech, his recent success was a welcome end to a very long and painful journey. Harr spent seven years writing his book, in which he tackled the difficult subject of a lawsuit brought on behalf of children and families suffering from cancer in clusters on Long Island, New York. Their cancer was caused by the toxic pollution of nearby industry. When he described the arduous task of beginning every day to work on the book, his description made writing *A Civil Action* sound like sheer torture. As I listened, I had an unpredictable reaction: I was ecstatic. A lightbulb went off in my head, and though I don't normally celebrate the misery of others, I remember thinking, "Oh, it's supposed to be hard. Hallelujah, maybe I can write after all!"

In this way, Jonathan Harr changed my life, because I began writing again the very next day and haven't stopped since. Not everyone has as torturous an experience as Harr, but all of us run into some rough spots now and then. We writers embrace the hard parts of writing, because there are so many rewarding experiences in the balance. As you write, you will have revelations and moments of nostalgia, creativity, and clarity that are so meaningful and fulfilling that you may even forget the difficult moments in between.

There are many tools and techniques you can utilize to minimize the work and help you through the challenges of writing your story. The next section provides some helpful ground rules to begin and maintain your writing so that you can avoid pitfalls and optimize your writing experience. If you adopt these ground rules, you will be ahead of the writing game from the very beginning.

THE GROUND RULES

The wise and practical author and teacher, Lois Daniel, provided her students with a list of ground rules to help them to overcome many of writing's difficult hurdles.[6] I believe this to be a very useful resource to facilitate writing, especially at the beginning. If you set out with a few clear, fundamental directives, you will be able to not only begin with more ease, but also continue with less uncertainty. And most importantly, you will more easily finish. After all, the goal is not simply to begin your life stories, but to finish them. So, I have followed Ms. Daniel's example and am offering a set of Ground Rules for you to follow. These are not exactly the same as the list Ms. Daniels provided in her book, *How to Write Your Own Life Story: The Classic Guide for the Nonprofessional Writer,* but they are most certainly inspired by it.

---

6 Lois Daniel. *How to Write Your Own Life Story: The Classic Guide for the Nonprofessional Writer,* Fourth Edition (Chicago: Chicago Review Press, 1997), 3–6.

1. Write the same as you speak.

Don't worry about style or how it sounds, just get your story down. When a writer begins writing, he or she knows to prioritize getting the story down first. So don't spend time correcting grammar or slang. Write down everything that comes to mind. You will have plenty of time for revision later.

2. Be yourself—not your celebrity version of yourself.

I will discuss in Chapter Five the mistaken temptation to write like your favorite famous author or celebrity. Tell your story as if you are relaying it to a friend, without affectation or what you think is marketable. When you remember to be yourself and set a goal to provide a story that is enjoyed by the folks who matter, your chances are much higher for success, both personally and commercially.

3. Truth is always best.

It's your story, and it must be told as you know it. However, make sure it is as truthful as you can remember. Lois Daniel said it best: "All good writing is an excursion into honesty." The exercise of writing your story is an opportunity to process what happened and what it meant to you. You can, of course, choose to leave out details that you do not want to disclose. But whatever you decide to include, make sure it is as honest as you can remember it. More about truth in Chapter Four.

4. *Think of your story as a living, breathing thing, not just as a timeline of events.*

Unless you are endeavoring to write a historical timeline, which is *not* a story, make sure you include your feelings and opinions. Relationships are always the core of a story, so include the people that are involved with your story and how you feel about them.

5. *Include humor.*

Whether you can retell incidents that were funny at the time or you were able to appreciate the humor of them in retrospect, include humor to add perspective and levity to your story. Even the most serious story can benefit from appropriate injections of humor.

6. *Include your lessons and your wisdom.*

Your story matters not simply because it happened. It matters because of the lessons, the wisdom, and the transcendence that you will share. There is a way to share the wisdom you've amassed in your life journey without being preachy. This should be your goal.

7. *Show, Don't Tell.*

This is especially important for setting the scene and for relaying feelings and emotions. Don't just tell your readers, "It was the best day of my life." Show them. Instead of proclaiming the occasion "dismal," illustrate why it was dismal. Also, the way you relay the lessons and wisdom discussed in Ground Rule #6 is to describe the circumstances that *illustrate* the lessons and the wisdom. This is how you avoid being preachy.

8. Create a Policy of Disclosure for Yourself.

Decide how much you want to tell about yourself and others. With your own disclosure policy in place, if you decide from the beginning that you do not want to delve too deeply into certain matters, or that you want to tell it all, then you've liberated yourself from having to decide each time the story begs the question of how much to tell. Caveat: be flexible with your policy. You may find that a deep disclosure feels right or that a little discretion on a certain matter feels better than you originally thought. It's always up to you.

9. Do Your Research.

The best way to avoid writer's block is with research. Whenever I am stuck on a story, I know that I have not fleshed out the facts enough. Often, since you are writing about yourself, you think the prose should always flow. But sometimes a snag happens where you don't feel you can go on. Just stop, go to your resources, check your facts and your sequences of events. Chances are, you have a gap in information or memory that is holding you back. Sometimes all you need is a slow stroll through your favorite photo album.

10. Read the stories of others.

Read *well-written* memoirs and autobiographies. They will help you identify some important elements of a good story and remind you of some of your own details to include in your writing. Your local library's biography section is brimming with enough choices to satisfy every taste. There are so many wonderful autobiographies, biographies, and memoirs on those library shelves that you may very well be overwhelmed with delight. I have included a list of recommended books in the Appendix to get you started. The stories of others should be considered part of your research resources.

As you are writing and editing, continue to check these Ground Rules and let them guide your process.

Story of a Girl:
A Little Girl and a Bully

"There you are, Little Miss Darling."

Every encounter with my bully started this same way. I cannot remember her name. But all these years later, I can still see her face—that sinister smile and those thin, arched eyebrows. Clear in my mind is how she wore her hair in two short pigtails that shot straight out in opposite directions like sparse bundles of dark twigs, over her ears. She was a tall, straight prepubescent rod of a girl.

She always found me during recess, but at no particular time or place in the span of those interminable forty minutes. She'd just appear, always when I least expected her, as if she knew the precise moment when I let my guard down. And it wasn't every day. So, I never figured out how to hide or where not to be. This second-grade version of myself always felt trapped, like a small, helpless animal, a hapless mouse in the paws of an alley cat, perhaps.

She would call me "Little Darling" or some other endearment, so sweetly, as she stroked my hair and wrapped one of my braids around her finger. For that first brief moment, her friendly, almost sisterly tone always tricked me. I didn't have an older sister, so I was not adept at knowing the difference between greetings that were sincere concern versus sardonic harbingers of doom. I was ever hopeful that the encounter would end as sweetly as it began.

To anyone else on the playground, near or passing by, she must have looked like an older admirer, maybe even a doting older sister. But by the time she had her finger completely entangled in my braid, all the way up to the hair band, she would begin to pull down, with increasing vigor, until I fell to the ground. If I hadn't fallen dramatically enough for her satisfaction, she'd give my hair a final quick and violent yank. Then I'd be on my hands and knees looking down at the tops of her white uniform Oxford shoes.

She always had the same friend with her. This girl was rounder, softer, and kinder. And though she would never stop my bully, she'd admonish her. "Don't do that to that little girl," she'd say with an inflection that sounded to me like she was both sympathetic and amused at the same time. "She ain't done nothin' to you."

My bully would only reply with a silent, cruel grin, and then demand that I stand. "Get up, cutie pie," she would say, all of the feigned sweetness gone from her tone. But I would stay right where I was, because she would have moved the toe of her white Oxford shoe over my fingers pinning them to the playground asphalt.

"See?" she'd say to her friend, "She won't even do as I say. She's a bad little girl. She is not obedient."

"Why don't you get up?" The friend would bend over and whisper. But by the time her mouth had reached my ear, my bully would have quickly slid her shoe away from my fingers. I would get up then and the friend would turn to my bully with another look of admonition, as if she had demonstrated how to get my cooperation. And the two of them would giggle face-to-face and then turn and walk away, blending back into the chaos of the playground, as if returning to some other dimension. It was then that my tears would well up. They came not from the pain in my fingers, or the humiliation of being forced onto my hands and knees. The tears, I believe now, signaled a mixture of helplessness and relief. I was happy to have survived another encounter, which seemed doubtful moments earlier. My bully always found me alone, and every moment I spent in the presence of her and her friend was frighteningly solitary and isolating. There would be no help, and because the feeling of hopelessness was so profound, I didn't tell anyone. I was so afraid of my bully that I couldn't see past the fear to reach out for protection.

This was the nature of the playground. The playground of my early years in Catholic school was the one place we kids were able to escape the nuns' strict rules and eagle eyes of judgment. And so I had to choose with whom I would align myself—with the grown folks or with the kids. I, in my shy, unprotected second-grade state, felt the risks were much too high to engage the nuns in this, my bully dilemma. I was too young and new to the playground to chance alienating the other kids. And so I remained silent about my bully until . . . well, until now, really.

WHAT MATTERS MOST IN CHAPTER TWO

1. Commit to starting with one story at a time. You are not required to start at the beginning.

2. One meaningful way to start can be with a turning-point story: somewhere in your childhood where "the door opens and lets in the future."

3. Writing is hard. But don't let that stop you!

4. Let the Ground Rules guide you and clarify your writing. Revisit them as you progress.

CHAPTER THREE

My Mother's Lessons: Writing About Mother

"In a child's eyes, a mother is a goddess. She can be glorious or terrible, benevolent or filled with wrath, but she commands love either way. I am convinced that this is the greatest power in the universe."

—N. K. Jemisin, The Hundred Thousand Kingdoms

"Fathers. Mothers. With all their caring and attention. They will fuck you up, every time."

—Chuck Palahniuk, Snuff

Speaking of bullies, I am frightened to death that my five children will one day write about their mother. Deep down, I know that because I have written so much about them as a parenting blogger and author, they will have their turns. I believe in karmic reciprocity. Also, I am certain that at least one of my children will pursue writing as a career, and when he or she does and when the idea of a memoir begins to be a pulsating beacon on his or her writing radar, the notion of mother-as-subject will surely follow. I have often marveled that my children seem to know me better than anyone else, even my husband, even my own mother. And I am often shocked and mortified by their scathing perception of my actions and my intentions. They are ruthless observers and unsentimental critics. They remember far more than I ever will . . . like what happened yesterday. And since there are five of them, they are their own community with a collective memory that is far more dangerous than each individual's. They have bonded in a way that excludes my husband and me, precisely because the very fibers of their bond are made up of their shared survival of their upbringing. Despite my best efforts, my children will, I suspect, have plenty to write about.

On the other hand, I have written about my mother many times, both in fiction and nonfiction. You will find at least one story about her in this book. My mother managed to raise me without any noteworthy drama or discord—no abuse or trauma. I had a happy childhood in a sanctuary of a household with two successfully married parents, who remained gainfully employed until retirement. In the child-rearing race, my mother and father reached the finish line with their healthy and optimistic notions of the world intact. Some would argue that this is why I am not a better writer. The craft of memoir writing seems to be best mastered by people whose childhoods held at least some form of well-entrenched dysfunction. And many writers, a disproportionate number, lay their family's dysfunction squarely at the feet of their mothers.

There are so many published mother memoirs that I could open up a bookstore, if it were currently prudent to do such a thing. I could call it About Mom and sell mother memoirs exclusively, with such a large inventory of choices that books would spill out of the front door. Often, writers begin their stories with no intention of writing about their mothers. Lori Gottlieb says as much about her memoir, *Stick Figure: A Diary of My Former Self:* "It's not that I set out to write about my mother," Gottlieb says. "It's just that it's virtually impossible to write about your childhood without writing about your mother, and people who grow up to be writers generally have some less than flattering observations to share."[7]

In *Mom & Me & Mom*, the late Maya Angelou has written a memoir about her life with and without her mother. Her mother left her with her grandmother as a child, where she remained until she was an adolescent. Some of the stories Angelou tells in this writing have already been shared in other books, but in this classic mother memoir, she spins her own story to include her mother's profound influence. Angelou's Vivian Baxter is a small woman with a humongous presence. She is a complicated character, full of contradictions and yet a powerful river of consistency who flows through Angelou's life, keeping her buoyed and moving forward, through loss and triumph. Angelou says of her mother:

---

7 Lori Gottlieb, "Mother, Brace Yourself," *New York Times Sunday Book Review*, May 7, 2009. Available online at: http://www.nytimes.com/2009/05/10/books/review/Gottlieb-t.html.

My mother's gifts of courage to me were both large and small. The latter are woven so subtly into the fabric of my psyche, I can hardly distinguish where she stops and I begin.

The mother figure does loom large over our lives. She most often casts a long and heavy shadow on her children, and the color of that shadow, bright or dark, is mostly permanent. In his book, *New Ways to Kill Your Mother: Writers and Their Families*, Colm Tóibín presents a tour de force of parental influence with his collection of essays exploring how writers' relationships with their families affect and inform their writing. In his essay, "Jane Austen, Henry James and the Death of the Mother," Tóibín suggests that the overbearing presence of mothers, as either controlling or coddling forces, interferes with the emergence of the protagonist's self-identity and is an obstacle to his or her independence. And so, he reasons, the author who seeks to develop a fully formed and engaged character must do away with the character's mother. Tóibín says, "Mothers get in the way in fiction; they take up space that is better filled by indecision; by hope; by the slow growth of a personality; and by something more interesting and important as the novel itself develops." Tóibín focuses this essay on novels of the eighteenth and nineteenth centuries, but we continue to see this theme in modern stories. The Disney lineup thoroughly illustrates this point. Disney kills off parents left and right in their feature films as the primary precursor to moving the protagonist from child to adult. Cinderella's mother dies when she is very young, and her weak and impotent father replaces mother with evil stepmother. Snow White's mom meets a similar fate. And I still cry when circus evildoers take Dumbo's mother away to elephant jail, and when Bambi's strapping buck of a father dies in that forest fire. In *The Lion King*, Simba's father's commanding James Earl Jones voice cannot save him from fratricide. And in *The Princess and the Frog*, Tiana loses her role-model father to overwork and poverty. These fairy tales acknowledge that we will be our parents' children all the way up to the moment that they are gone. And only then are we on our own.

And so it is no wonder that we are compelled to write about our mothers. They are the sun around whom we orbit. Their influence is so profound as to be avoidable only in death. And even then, avoidance is not so certain.

When it comes to writing about your mother for purposes of your life story, you must remember that it is *your* story. You are not writing your mother's life story, but rather your story of your mother. These two are not the same, nor should they be. And though you may feel compelled to have your mother read your story to check facts, or maybe to get her blessing or critique, ultimately it is your version of things. So give yourself the freedom to write all that you want to say or that comes to you by simply remembering that you are only speaking for yourself and that even if you wanted to include the perspective of others, that perspective is still filtered through yours. Part of the power and purpose of writing your own stories is that you are getting down your unique experience from your viewpoint. By embracing this power, you are also freeing yourself from the burden of speaking for or on behalf of others. Even once you've mined your memory and the memory of others by gathering your own and stories from family and friends, scoured Ancestry.com, gathered your photo albums and letters, and aligned your facts and quotes and had them verified in all ways possible, what is ultimately written is your version.

With the freedom to write anything that is uniquely from your perspective, you still must refrain from trying to write everything. The subject of what you should include and what you should not is BIG. And you will find it impossible to avoid what I call the Four Horsemen of Disclosure.

THE FOUR HORSEMEN OF DISCLOSURE: INCLUSION, EXCLUSION, DISCRETION, AND TRUTH

When it comes to disclosure, there are subtle but important differences between the four big-picture questions: What to include? What to leave out? When and where is discretion necessary and merciful? Is it true?

Inclusion involves focus. Exclusion requires editing. Discretion engages an interplay of compassion and empathy. And truth is the overriding principle to which all memoir writing must adhere. Truth is so important as to deserve its own chapter, thus Chapter Four.

Often the most difficult task in writing is not deciding what to include, but what to leave out. Your life, and all of the facts and figures, themes and incidences therein, can—

especially at the onset of your efforts—be an overwhelming smorgasbord of story possibilities. This is why you are narrowing your focus to one story at a time. Before you begin to write, ask yourself a two-part inquiry. Part one: what is the theme that you want to share—forgiveness, redemption, discovery of a gift, courage in the face of loss, perseverance? These are what I mean by theme. If your answer is "my life," or "my childhood," your focus is too broad. So you must narrow it down to what you want to relay to others about your life or your childhood. Then once you know the theme, part two of the inquiry is: what is the illustration of that theme? Once you can answer the theme and illustration questions, you must pick the tidbits and only those tidbits that drive *that* story forward.

Marion Roach Smith, in *The Memoir Project: A Thoroughly Non-Standardized Text for Writing and Life,* says it nicely. She suggests that when you are clear about your theme, "[t]his is what you are now allowed to do—to glide into the banquet that is your tale and take what you need from the feast." We will revisit the importance of careful picking and choosing when I discuss the editing process in Chapter Six. But as you are writing your first draft, you must remain clear about what your story is about and not get waylaid or bogged down in the ocean of details that may not be important.

Now there is a caveat: between theme and illustration, sometimes the illustration is much clearer in your mind than the theme. In fact, there may be many themes in your story, even in its tightest form. When this is true, you can back into the two-part inquiry. Recently, my business partner, Carol, and I were discussing a story she had written about her mother. I had already read her story when I asked her what her story was about. She answered that her story was a love story that she had illustrated through a story of a duck. I agreed that it was a love story, but more specifically, I thought the story was about the affection between her and her mother, and between her and all of her family and friends who supported her through the ordeal of her mother's death. The duck was not an illustration, the events surrounding her mother's death were the illustration. The duck was a device that she carried throughout the story to represent her mother's involvement in her life. She acknowledged that she came to her analysis—that the story was a love story—in hindsight. However, when she started the story, she knew she wanted to talk about her mother and the support of her family. And she knew she wanted to tell the story of the duck. If she was not clear about those goals and instead just had her mind set on a "love story," she may have been all over the map.

So the two-part inquiry consists of questions to help you maintain a tight story. However, you can back into your focus. And this is how: if you know the answer to the second question—"How will I illustrate my story?"—then before you begin, examine exactly what you are illustrating, asking "What am I trying to say with this illustration?" In this way, you can articulate for yourself just what is important about that illustration and, thus, key to the story.

The third horseman of disclosure, discretion, represents the challenging question of how much personal business of yours and others do you want to tell. When you open up about yourself and those persons who are a part of your

story, you don't want to tease your reader with shallow out-
lines of your characters. It is important to be truthful and
thorough.

Ground Rule #7 asks you to show and not just tell. This
means that your illustrations need not only be descriptive,
but they also need to be whole and without gaps. If you were
painting a picture, you would not want portions to be filled
in with vibrant color and clear delineations, while other parts
are only outlined in charcoal. However, the depths of candor
and disclosure are up to you. Recently, for the inaugural epi-
sode of her new online show, *Red Table Talk*, Jada Pinkett-
Smith brought together her mother and her daughter for a
frank and open discussion about their lives. Her mother,
Adrienne Banfield Jones, and Pinkett-Smith began an intimate conversation about Pinkett-Smith's upbringing. Jones
wanted to know if Pinkett-Smith had any resentment about
her childhood. At some point in the interaction, Pinkett-
Smith mentioned that the audience (including her daughter,
Willow) could not really understand the backdrop of her
childhood without knowing more about her mother's early
years. She then allowed Jones to tell as much about those
years as she was willing. Jones made the decision to disclose
that she gave birth to Pinkett-Smith when she was a teenager
and that she spent the majority of her daughter's developing
years addicted to drugs.

The ensuing discussion launched, in stellar fashion, what
Pinkett-Smith said she hoped would be real, in-depth dia-
logue. Both women showed that they were committed to this
vision: Pinkett-Smith and Jones hashed out their feelings
about a seminal part of their lives together, and Willow

heard part of her beloved grandmother's story for the first time. As a viewer, I felt as if I was sitting in on a private conversation where authentic emotions and sentiments were being openly and freshly expressed.

Pinkett-Smith, Jones, and Willow could have easily opted for a lighter glimpse into the multigenerational relationship between them. All three of them are lovely to watch, and taking in the similarities between the three was engaging enough to hold my attention. But they decided to go deeper. And because they did, I am still talking about the experience.

This is not to suggest that full disclosure is always the right decision. There have been plenty of times when I've read a story that goes too far into cringe-worthy territory, and I've thought, "Oh boy, that's too much information." But I mainly have that reaction when a writer has gone off subject and provided information that is not germane to the progress of the story.

In order to deal with this issue of disclosure, I respectfully refer you back to Ground Rule #8, which encourages you to set a disclosure policy for yourself. If you decide up front that you are going to either release the floodgates of truth or err on the side of a less-is-more approach, at least you've set your standard and freed yourself from having to decide with each turn of your story. Remember, however, to be flexible. If you find that you want to tell more of a certain part, or perhaps are willing to tell all when it comes to your actions but want to refrain from implicating someone else, give yourself the creative license to go with your gut.

A Short Mother Story:
The Woman and Her Shadow

The woman is tall and slender. She walks erect with dignity and poise. She is an intelligent woman. She is fashionable and charming. She is a beauty that halts conversation at cocktail parties when she enters, and makes passersby on the street stop, transfixed. They stop because she has broken their walking rhythm. She has caused them to misstep or run into something. When people see her, they are sure that she is someone famous. They are certain they have seen her on a magazine cover or on television. But this woman is oblivious to the stir she causes. The attention she draws is not her intention, nor her purpose, which makes her all the more alluring.

Now, if you look closely, if you are able to break free from your mesmerized gaze and look more discerningly at her, you will notice the woman's shadow. Her shadow is always with her regardless of the sun's position. Like most shadows, though, this shadow holds its own—also erect and walking pridefully, basking in the attention not intended for it, fully aware of the woman's impact on others, even though the woman is not. But unlike most shadows that stream behind a person, taller and bigger, this shadow is barely detectable behind the radiance of the woman. It is small and skinny, and it clings closely to her skirt. Nonetheless, the shadow is happy to belong to the woman, happy to be everywhere she is.

The woman, too, is happy for the company of the shadow. They are a content pair.

The woman is my mother and the shadow is me.

I sometimes try to remember when I first realized that my mother was exceptional. All children, I think, possess conflicted notions of their mothers. She is simultaneously the most significant woman they know on the one hand and just Mom on the other. Perhaps the just Mom part comes later in adolescence. I think for most folks, the ambivalence about their mothers comes when they are teens and the cloud over their eyes clears. They begin to see their parents for the flesh-and-blood people they are. They are able to perceive their parents' mistakes and weaknesses, and thus the pedestal that parents occupy in their children's early-childhood eyes begins to crumble. Perhaps at the time that our own inner critic turns so mercilessly against us, we turn on our parents, too. I know this is true because it happened to me with regard to my father, but never my mother. I am not sure if the hyper-critic of my adolescence took a look and could not find any flaws in her, or if the childhood cloud of perfection just never cleared. In any case, her pedestal remains fully intact even now.

Often, in such cases, a girl would tend to use the perfection of her mother against herself, comparing and always falling short. But that didn't happen for me either. Much of that self-esteem work was done by my mother, who made me feel beautiful and exceptional and more fortunate than she. I remember wishing out loud that I was tall like she was. But she'd say, "You are the perfect height because I prayed to God that you would not have to suffer being tall the way I have. I had terrible growing pains, and my posture was atrocious. My pants were always too short. And I was taller than all of the boys. You are so lucky to be your perfect size."

When I complained about my pimples and how I wished my skin was as smooth as hers, she'd say, "Oh, when I was your age, I had the worst acne. I was that girl who was too big and whose face was 'unfortunate,' full of angry red acne all of the time. Those little blemishes you have will go away in no time. You are so lucky to have good skin."

And so I did feel lucky, even when outspoken friends and family commented that I was the spitting image of my father. As handsome as one's father may be, no girl wants to be his spitting image.

As my mother's shadow, I witnessed the power of beauty. How it works on your behalf, even before you open your mouth to speak. In those small, subtle ways, in the secret world of preference and bias, beauty arrives long before your intentions and paves the way—opens doors, clears paths, and puts "yes" on the lips of strangers. Everyone, men and women, want to please a beautiful woman. They want to solicit her smile, and they want to garner her approval. When my mother entered a department store, store clerks came out of the woodwork to assist her. The first time I wandered into a department store by myself, I braced myself for a barrage of overzealous offers of assistance, but they never came. In fact, no one spoke to me the entire time I shopped. The only attention I earned was from the not-so-subtly lurking lady in a burgundy store security blazer, who followed me at a distance until I left the store.

I watched my mother navigate through and around the conflicted nature of her friendships. If my mother were just beautiful, this would have been easier. But she also has a quick and easy wit. And she is astute and insightful in the way that smart people are astute and insightful. To make matters worse, she has impeccable taste. And so her friends wanted not just her looks, but also her look—everything about it: her clothes, her perfume, her furniture, her bedspread and curtains. All she had to do was say that she liked a design, a fabric, a color—and before the next weekend rolled around, my mother's choices appeared in her friends' homes.

Me, the shadow, watched all of this unfold and took it in as the normal course of things. As I got older, my mother increasingly endeavored to push me into my own light. Though I didn't resist, I never thought that I should try to aspire to be as wondrous as she, and she never pushed me to be. Most girls with exceptional mothers can choose the opposite thing to hang their own exceptionalism on: what their mothers are not. If your mother is a great beauty, you can be the great brain. If your mother is the great brain, you can cultivate your beauty. But when your mother was both homecoming queen and valedictorian, you have to shoot for something else. And searching for that something else can be, I am finding, a lifelong endeavor.

WHAT MATTERS MOST IN CHAPTER THREE

1. Take heart. Your experiences with your difficult mother will likely make you a better writer.

2. When you write about your mother, you are writing *your* story of your mother, not her own story.

3. Before you begin your story, clarify your theme and how you will illustrate your theme.

4. Show, don't tell. Be descriptive. Make sure the picture you are drawing with your words has clear delineations and vibrant colors.

5. Set a disclosure policy and don't break it . . . unless you need to.

CHAPTER FOUR

When and Where Love Enters

*"Whether or not you claim to be interested in it, from
the moment you are alive you are bound to be
concerned with love . . ."*
—Thomas Merton

We soon discover, as we travel down our life's road, that relationships are at the core of every conflict, at the root of every problem, and in the middle of every triumph and joy. Is it possible, then, to write our life stories without writing about love? Would we want to leave love out even if we could? No, we wouldn't and no, we couldn't. Lindsay Tigar, New York–based freelance writer, who has been writing about love for years, turned me onto the above quote by prolific author and Catholic mystic Thomas Merton, who also said love is "a completeness, a fullness, a wholeness of life." Perhaps it takes a contemplative, like Merton, to have and express such clarity on the matter. Possibly the rest of us are too mired in our relationships to be able to take a step back and see them for what they are: the most central theme and what makes our lives full and whole.

WRITING ROMANCE

Our romantic relationships provide the drama of life. Both Thalia and Melpomene, the Greek muses of comedy and tragedy—whose masks have long been the symbol of dramatic balance—both give a nod to stories about love, even though romance is its own genre. Love is almost always the mess in the middle of the comedic and the tragic. Romance Writers of America defines the romance genre as requiring essentially two basic elements: a central love story and an emotionally satisfying and optimistic ending.[8] We know that the second element, an emotionally satisfying and optimistic ending, does not necessarily mean a happy ending, otherwise *Romeo and Juliet* and *Love Story* would not qualify. So, an optimistic ending must indicate that the boy gets the girl or the girl gets the boy, and of course, there's that till-death-do-us-part part. Jane Austen's *Pride and Prejudice* continues to thrill readers as the quintessential classic of romantic literature. My youngest daughter has a tattered copy of this book on her nightstand, as I write.

Truth is, romance novels are the most popular genre in modern literature, comprising almost 55 percent of all pa-

---

8 Romance Writers of America®, http://www.rwa.org/p/cm/ld/fid=578.

perback books sold in 2004. The runaway popularity of *Fifty Shades of Grey* demonstrates that romance is much sought after, especially if it is served up with a hefty helping of steamy sex. The *Fifty Shades of Grey* series has singlehandedly rebirthed a romance subgenre, wherein all of the elements of romance are combined with explicit eroticism. The end result has women rushing to their local bookstores to sweep up *Fifty Shades* to the tune of forty million copies sold thus far. The first book has become the fastest-selling paperback of all time, surpassing *Harry Potter.*

Romantic entanglements are also the lifeblood of cinema and television. Almost every genre must share the screen with romance to some degree. Even the television shows whose promoted themes are not romantic, such as crime and medical dramas, center their stories on intense relationships—like Maddie Hayes and David Addison of *Moonlighting,* Scully and Mulder of *The X-Files,* and Temperance Brennan and Seeley Booth of *Bones.* The same-sex buddy-partners of *Starsky and Hutch, Rizzoli and Isles,* and *Beavis and Butt-Head* personify the intensely evolving relationships that at least resemble romantic couplings—they're not called bromances for nothing! It's easy to see that reality shows are absolutely built on romantic alliances and dalliances, as are their precursors: soap operas.

Of all the stories we crave, love stories reign supreme. I believe that part of our attraction to the romantic stories of others—in fiction as well as nonfiction, in books as well as in movies, television shows and music—is a hunger to learn how to govern our own relationships. When we are growing up, rarely do we receive deliberate instruction on romance.

So we have to pick up clues and cues about how to love and be loved from watching our parents and the other adults around us, and from the media. Since our romances are the beginning of our pursuits for lifelong mates, we yearn to know how to get it right.

When you endeavor to share your own true love stories with others, you should feel no pressure to change your story if it is not exactly a shining example of relationship gone right. Often, the most interesting stories are of love gone way to the other side of wrong. These stories hold their own valuable lessons, too. I mention romantic fiction to point out that the public hungers for romance and love stories, both the optimistic, happy-ending kind, and the difficult, not so beautifully resolved kind. And people need to read real accounts to counterbalance the fantasy.

With our own love stories, we really must not try to compete with the likes of the fictional accounts offered up in *Fifty Shades of Grey* or those we see on television. A person could hurt herself trying to achieve that! Instead, we will have truth on our side. And everyone knows that often, especially when it comes to drama, conflict, and the complexity of love, truth can be stranger, more twisted, or sweeter and more poignant, than fiction.

Intertwined in Cheryl Strayed's *Wild*, the memoir of her solo thousand-mile hike along the Pacific Crest Trail, is the story of her marriage unraveling and her own extramarital affairs that precipitated her divorce. The loss of her seminal relationships (the traumatic early death of her mother, her sexual exploits with near-strangers, and a post-breakup alliance with a heroin addict) send her plummeting to her life's rock bottom and motivate her ill-prepared trek through the Western wilderness all alone. Her love stories are harrowing and heartbreaking. And so she walks and hikes through one adventure (and misadventure) to another, buoyed by the tenuous ties to the people of her past and the new connections she makes along her way. Through it all, she experiences a kind of recovery and healing that has inspired many readers to follow in her footsteps. There are, as I write, aspiring Pacific Crest Trail hikers running to REI in hopes of capturing for themselves some part of Strayed's soul-shifting transformation for themselves.

In her book, *Paris: A Love Story*, Kati Marton, foreign correspondent turned author, shares the story of the loves of her life, who happened to be high-profile famous folk: journalistic giant Peter Jennings and American diplomatic legend Richard Holbrooke. Her story is rich, with about as much romance, drama, and tragedy as any story can contain. In them, we learn about her passionate and difficult marriage to Jennings, who, she says, was insecure, difficult, and moody. (Who knew?) And we get a peek at the complications of their small family during his illness and last days. Marton also tells of her exciting life as the wife of a Washington insider: the quiet way she and Holbrooke found each other, and the frenetic public life she lived as the confidant to the globetrotting, crisis-abating diplomat. The fact that Marton's love stories are true makes them all the more compelling.

And so, let's spend a moment considering the importance of truth, that Fourth Horseman of Disclosure.

Telling the Truth

"So remember: The writer of memoir makes a pact with her reader that what she writes is the truth as best she can tell it. But the original pact, the real deal, is with herself. Be honest, dig deep, or don't bother."

—Abigail Thomas, *Thinking About Memoir*

Number three of the Ground Rules in Chapter Two strongly suggests that you commit yourself to telling the truth in your writing. With her stern advice (above) to "dig deep or don't bother," Abigail Thomas is trying to get at something deeper than the ethics of truth telling. Yes, it's important to deliver the real story if you've promised it. But you must also commit yourself to facing your story and grappling with it. The process of getting your story down is one that promises to change you. As you contemplate where you have been and what you have done, as you grasp at the meaning and the lessons of your life, you have the opportunity to embark on a journey of discovery. This is an opportunity to clarify for yourself who you are, what your purpose has been, and what it is now. If, instead of processing the truth, you are preoccupied with formulating a fictional account—or worse, re-envisioning a more savory result—you are really cheating yourself.

The other side of truth that is also important to remember is that, when it comes to occurrences in one's history, truth can be subjective. And there are many levels to the subjectivity of truth. In any given situation, one person's perspective of how things happened may differ widely from the person who stood side-by-side with the observer as things went down. The adage "no two stories are alike" is true. In addition, our own grasp of what happened during events in our past can change. Our minds have many filters. And when we experience an event, those filters significantly impact the final version that we store in our memory banks.

Jonathan Gottschall suggests in his book, *The Storytelling Animal*, that a healthy human mind manipulates events in order to preserve a positive self-image. We all want to be the protagonists in our own stories, thus we have a difficult time portraying ourselves as the bad guy. Important to our mental health, Gottschall says, is our ability to see ourselves with redeeming qualities. And this need affects how we see all things. As a result, he points out through study findings, although we have great confidence in our memories, our memories are far from reliable. And with regard to our life stories, Gottschall says:

A life story is a carefully shaped narrative that is replete with strategic forgetting and skillfully spun meanings.

As such, Gottschall suggests that when we endeavor to write our life stories, we should include the disclaimer: "This story that I tell about myself is only based on a true story. It is in large part a figment of my own yearning imagination." Marion Roach Smith also suggests including a disclaimer along with your memoirs that states simply, "Here's how I see it," or "Here's how it happened to me." Accepting the subjectivity of your own view does not discredit your version in any way. To the contrary, you can fully acknowledge that your story is how you experienced events and fully own it without fearing its differences from the experiences of others. Embracing this approach comes in handy, especially when writing about family and other relationships.

The most striking example I can offer of the malleability of truth is the story of my earliest memory as a child: my parents' wedding. This event sticks out in my mind as one of the most exciting days of my life. I was three years old. I remember sitting in a crowded church. I was very happy to be all dressed up and a part of things. Weddings are a universe of nervous energy, pomp, circumstance, flowers, and beauty. In the eyes of a small girl child, the combination of these markers of importance—women in full makeup and regalia, men in bow ties, glowing candles, fragrant rose petals, and crowded church pews—signal that something of the utmost significance is about to happen. My mother was, of course, all done up. On that day, she was the tallest woman to grace the aisle. And that seemed fitting, since it was her moment. My father was his most turned out. As far as I can remember, my father, quite the snappy dresser almost always, has been this supremely dapper on only two occasions: his wedding and mine.

I was sitting on someone's lap (whose lap I cannot recall), oddly in the middle of a pew in the middle of the church, quite a distance from the front. I could not really see all that was happening at the altar, and I could not hear the proceedings. The church was midsize as far as Catholic churches go, and the year had to be 1965. I sat among quite tall people and missed most of the vow-making, ring-exchanging, and kissing-the-bride parts. But the clearest memory I can still recollect all these decades later is my parents walking briskly down the aisle together and out of the heavily carved church doors into the bright sunlight outside.

In the years that followed this event, I would often share the experience with others—family, friends, and even strangers. And it is this propensity to share indiscriminately that forced my mother to step in with the truth, which is that I did not attend my parents' wedding at all. The wedding that I am remembering was the wedding of their closest friends, Jean and Willie. This was devastatingly disappointing to me as an eight-year-old when my mother finally sat me down to straighten this out. Evidently, she had tried to tell me the truth before I was eight, but I didn't allow it to really sink in until then.

"Honey, you were not at your Dad's and my wedding!" she said gently.

"Yes, I was!" I replied with the full confidence of youth.

"No, sweetheart. You were not born when we were married. You came three years after."

"Then whose wedding was it, and why were you wearing a wedding dress? And why were you carrying a bouquet?"

"I wasn't in a wedding dress, sweet. I was the matron of honor in Jean's wedding, and I was wearing a midnight-blue bridesmaid dress. Bridesmaids and matrons get to hold small bouquets, too, sometimes."

"But Daddy came down the aisle with you."

"Yes, he was the best man."

"Oh."

It is quite romantic for a girl to think that she witnessed the most important marriage in her family's history. And so I was quite dismayed that the bride and groom were not my parents. But more than just dismayed, I was terribly wrong about how I remembered things. Very recently, when I was testing out the very first writing prompt for our "Story of a Girl" writing workshop, I contemplated the question, "What is your earliest memory?"

And this parents'-wedding-that-wasn't-really-their-wedding memory came up. Since it is my earliest recollection of childhood and still quite clear in my mind, I called both my mother and the bride, Jean, to compare my memories with their facts. Certain details in my head would not make sense in the full light of truth. For example, in my memory, the wedding took place in our family church, the midsize, Catholic church that I've already mentioned. However, Jean assures me that the wedding actually happened in a small neighborhood Baptist church located on the other side of town. Did her Baptist church have large, heavily carved doors? Nope. Was my mother wearing white? Of course not. And it makes perfect sense that I would be in a pew in the middle of the church instead of at the front. I was likely sitting on my grandmother's lap. It is true that my mother was the tallest woman in the church and that my parents walked swiftly down the aisle past me, hand-in-hand, in marital bliss . . . just not as the sparkling newlyweds of my story.

So it can be with memories. They are truth sprinkled with a little pixie dust, and not just the pixie dust of time. They are sprinkled with the pixie dust of wishful thinking and youthful fancy. And over the years, you might expect the

vision to get fuzzy. To the contrary, my memories had so-
lidified the fancy into fact. This is what we must acknowledge when we write our stories. When I am writing the story
of my earliest memory, I can either write the truth, or I can
write the "truth" of my memory, as I have just done here. My
earliest memory story as I have further explained it here is
what I get when I take the memories in my head and adjust
them by what I have discovered through research. If I were to
write only the memory the way my nostalgic inner child
wants to remember it, I would knowingly be writing fiction.
If I put forth this story as fact, a disclaimer would not suffice.
I now know my version to be faulty. You must tell the truth
as you know it, and fact-checking is *always* a good idea.

Even though, as Gottschall says, we are "figments of our
own imaginations," and "heroes of our own epics," there is a
difference between sharing your own truth and creating an
embellished story out of laziness or for the sake of popularity.
Examples abound of best-selling nonfiction that turned out
to be fiction. James Frey, author of the now infamous *A Million Little Pieces*, has been the poster child of fraudulent memoirs ever since Oprah Winfrey outed him about his untruths.
May he stand as a beacon to remind us that lying is costly to
your credibility and that embellishing your story defeats your
purpose of getting your truth in print. Writers who opt for
the sensational over the truthful sell their readers short.
Marion Roach Smith so eloquently advises writers to "value
the reader, whose hunger for truth is enormous and whose
thirst for understanding this life is unquenchable."

When you are in a story crunch—as in, seized in the
middle of your story with an information lapse that halts

everything—or you feel like your story is not sexy or compelling, stop yourself and repeat these four words three times: "My truth is enough. My truth is enough. My truth is enough."

The Beginning of a Love Story: Marriage by June

Jon and I are strolling familiar ground. The mall is often where we go when we are home from college and visiting my parents. We have been dating for six months, and we have already visited this mall together enough that Jon knows its landscape, as if he were the one who grew up in my hometown. He is walking with purpose today, pulling me along by the hand. This is unusual because I am most often walking faster than and slightly ahead of him. But not today. Today, with a quickened pace, he is pulling me toward the jewelry store. We enter and are greeted by a tall woman who looks to be in her early sixties. Her hair is styled in a high, blond bouffant and her eyebrows heavily filled in with black pencil. She is wearing a black-and-white blouse that accentuates her large bosom, broad shoulders, and the curve of her waist. She smiles widely and says with a warm exuberance, "Oh, you're back! And you've brought someone with you."

"Yes," Jon says, "we're here to make a decision, hopefully." He is using his formal voice, and he is wearing that nervous smile he wore when he asked me to dance that very first time at a college dorm party.

"And who is this lovely young lady?" asks the woman.

"This is Gina. . . ."

"And she is your fiancée? Your future bride?"

"Yes," Jon's voice cracks, and his mood shifts from nervousness to embarrassment. "I am not used to saying that yet."

"And that is why you need a ring, my dear. A sparkling new engagement ring will speak for you." The woman turns her focus to me. I am flabbergasted that Jon has been to this store without me, shopping for a ring. I am amazed that he has turned all of our talk of marriage into clandestine action. He did ask me to marry him, but the proposal was somewhat casual, like the nearly off-hand way you might mention marriage instead of just saying "I love you" yet another time. Between two college students with idealistic and tentative life plans and no money, asking the question is safe, not so serious. And saying yes as I did, the same.

I wonder if the jewelry store woman knows I am not yet twenty and he is just twenty-one. By today's standards, we are still children. But in this engagement ring store, the degree of Jon's seriousness engulfs me for the first time, and I know that this sweet man with no money and no solid plan, except evidently this one, really loves me. He wants to make our engagement official and put our love on the map.

"Now, then, Miss Gina. I am June Garibaldi," June says with a strong and unapologetic Southern drawl. "Your sweetheart has been here doing his homework." June leads me over to the glass counter. She goes around to stand behind it and pulls a ring of keys out of her skirt pocket.

"And I have to say, he has exquisite taste!" She puts a selection of five rings nestled in their lofty navy-blue velvet beds onto the counter. I turn to Jon with wide eyes and mouth agape. He is smiling that shy, self-conscious smile that makes me swoon and blush each time he wears it, even thirty years later. As it turns out, Jon does have exquisite taste in jewelry. From this beginning point of our engagement until now, I have been the primary beneficiary of Jon's delight in exercising this inexplicable gift with jewelry. If you have the power to request a trait in your mate, I highly recommend that you choose a man who has good taste in jewelry. I am lucky in this. It was a thrilling discovery.

On this day in the jewelry store, Jon is wearing a sports jersey and jeans. His muscles are contorting his jersey in ways that announce to the world that he is a football player and bodybuilder. I am wearing a pink-and-green polo shirt and some old jeans, and it occurs to me that I should be dressed better for this occasion—a flattering dress, heels, a little more makeup! But I am dressed for a stroll in the mall, not for a milestone moment in our history together.

Jon and I met in the first week of my freshman year in college. He was with a group of football players I encountered on my way back from registering for classes. One of the other players called out to me by name, even though we had never met. I was freshly new on campus, having arrived only two days before. This friend of Jon's had taken note of me in the Froshbook, which is a picture book of all incoming freshmen. Upperclassmen used the book, I learned later, as a kind of dating prospect preview, if they can get their hands on it early. This boy took this chance encounter as an opportunity to flirt, and he was acting as if he knew me. He introduced me to the group as if we were friends or more. I thought this stranger was odd, a bit creepy, and not a little bit obnoxious. Jon knew what his friend was up to, and he deliberately removed himself from this awkward introduction by taking a step back and slightly behind the others. Because of this, I did not really make note of him. He seemed to be trying to disappear, and so I let him. In fact, it took a few more encounters before we actually exchanged words. I danced with him at parties and saw him in the bookstore on occasion. But these were brief crossings. It was when we went on a double date to his fraternity's spring formal that I came to appreciate who he was. A friend who sang with me in the gospel choir asked me to the formal. He was Jon's fraternity brother. Jon's date was a freshman like me and a friend of my date.

As we were waiting for a table at a very crowded San Francisco restaurant, I found Jon to be the most captivating person in the building. He was wearing a handsome gray suit, with a pink shirt and a narrow tie with pink-and-navy-blue stripes. His tie was very current and trendy. He looked good in his suit. Dapper. He was matching his date's pink dress. She was in a sour mood because they got lost on the way to the restaurant, and she expressed to the group she didn't like Jon's tie. As we waited for our table, Jon brought his date some kind of frothy drink from the bar that matched the color of her dress and his shirt. His date rejected the peace offering with a wave of her hand, and so, Jon made a toast—Cheers!—and drank the drink himself. His date greeted the toast with a scowl. The humor and charm of the gesture was not lost on me, however.

My date was dressed very conservatively. His tie was wide and his suit pristine but dated, reminding me (affectionately) of my granduncle's funeral suit. My date was in good spirits and as the planner of the evening, he had gone out of his way to organize a fun night. Still, I was totally distracted by Jon. I tried not to stare as I took him in, his snappy suit and tie and his silly sense of humor. His deep voice resonated pleasantly, and he smelled good—no cologne, just soap and deodorant and youthful masculinity. As we were escorted to our table, I had a fleeting wish that we could swap dates. But no swap occurred. We were reasonable people, above all. He called me the next day.

To my untrained and uncultivated eyes, the five rings Jon has chosen are all lovely. I love each one mostly because Jon came here without me and picked them out on his own. I am especially fond of the one that fits between two bands sort of like a puzzle. When I pick this ring out, June removes it from its bed and puts it on my finger. Then she takes it off and replaces it, one after the other, with the remaining choices. The rings are beautiful on my hand, even though my knuckles are dry and my fingernail polish is chipped. But I am certain that the puzzle ring is my favorite.

June asks me if I'd like to see any other rings from their exhaustive collection, but I say no. I love the puzzle ring and the idea of combing through all of the others overwhelms me. So I choose this ring, one of the choices that Jon chose first. And I have never regretted it. It occurred to me in that moment in the jewelry store, influenced by my newly dawning feminist awareness, that I should not begin this marital relationship deferring to my husband in this way. This, I am thinking, is a sign of weakness and traditional usurpation of power. And in the midst of this thought it also occurs to me that someone has to pay for this ring and neither of us has any money. When Jon sits down and begins to fill out the credit paperwork, another coming-of-age milestone happens: Jon jumps into debt on my behalf. And this "feminist" young woman he decides he wants to marry lets him.

June gently guides Jon into scraping up a bigger down payment and signing in blood onto a payment plan committing income that he does not yet have. It is a sobering and serious moment. And June is patient and kind. She is both firm and reassuring. It feels as if she is not just selling us a ring. She is presiding expertly over a transition. We are really doing this, growing up in the jewelry store. And so in an ever so slightly less romantic mood, we leave June Garibaldi feeling more in love, more deeply committed, and newly in debt.

Only the truly optimistic need bother with marriage. I know for a fact that I was more in love than I was prepared for the rigors of married life. But the rigors don't look like rigors early on because they are couched in hope and promise and possibility, just like those sparkling rings in their velvet beds. Marriage requires one of you to be the initiator, and the initiator must be both the braver and the most optimistic.

I am lucky that Jon is that—the brave one, the optimistic one, the romantic one, the risk-taker, and the closer. And I suppose to counter this Christopher Columbus personality, there must be a Queen Isabella to provide motivation and support, to say "Yes. Okay, let's do this!" I fancy myself a Queen Isabella, both muse and enabler. One of my parents' favorite stories from my childhood speaks to this, sort of. After watching a professional football game on television (back when families watched their one television set together), my brother, no older than seven years old and very inspired by the heroics unfolding on the screen, proclaimed, "When I grow up, I am going to be a football player!" To this, I, at four or five, jump up and added: "And I'll be the people!" My parents and my grandfather think this is very funny and endearing. They laugh very hard in that moment and tell the story many times, until I get older and come to feel that it is a shameful display of low self-esteem. I pray that they'll stop telling it. And fortunately, the story gets replaced with something funnier, perhaps stronger of character. But later, I begin to feel that the statement is not completely without merit as a life goal: to boost up and support my loved ones in their endeavors. I've come to know that this can only be accomplished effectively from a place of influence and authority. Queen Isabella was, after all, no shrinking violet. If one of my daughters proclaimed that she wanted to be "the people" right now, I would likely gasp. But then I'd take a deep breath and suggest that there are many levels to this: you can be "the people" as in a fan, or you can be "the people" as in the owner of the football team. It's okay to endeavor to be both.

My not-quite-twenty-year-old-newly-engaged self would agree, I think. But to the question—should a couple get married at the youthful and naive ages of not yet twenty and twenty-one?—With thirty years of hindsight and a marriage that is still a work in progress, my answer must be: only if among you there is a Christopher Columbus, a Queen Isabella, and maybe a June Garibaldi.

What Matters Most in Chapter Four

1.   The world craves a good love story. "Good" doesn't necessarily mean happy, so don't be compelled to leave out the messy, not-so-neat or beneficially resolved parts.

2.   Truth is subjective, but do your best to be truthful and honest.

3.   Fact-check.

4.   Recognize that your story is as close to the truth as your delicate ego will allow. But knowingly lying cheats your readers and yourself. If you want to make up a story, write fiction.

CHAPTER FIVE

Your Testimony

"A testimony is pain that has been reassigned."
—Johnnie Dent, Jr.

THE DIFFERENT WAYS WE TESTIFY

A testimony is a story that chronicles a spiritual or religious experience: how a person came to encounter God, the Spirit, or a profound life-changing truth. Even though types of testimony span a broad array of subject and themes, I have always been most intrigued by religious conversions. History is chock full of these intense and often abrupt upheavals in belief. They happen in every spiritual discipline and make for popular life stories. When a person decides to change from one religion to another, he or she has chosen nothing less than a personal revolution. A convert rejects an old belief system and embraces new ways of governing her life. And she is likely leaving behind a social structure that she fully knows—relationships with potentially whole communities of people—and stepping into a new and different one.

I most enjoy the stories from people who are (or at least appear to be) at the top of their spiritual game when they are moved to switch up and change teams. My favorite story from the *Bible*, not surprisingly, is the story of the Apostle Paul's conversion to Christianity. At the time Paul was knocked off his high horse and struck blind by Christ, he was not only devoutly Jewish, but he was a zealous persecutor of early Christian followers. In fact, Chapter Nine of Acts in the New Testament says he was on his way to Damascus to find that bothersome cult of religious revolutionaries and put an end to it, one misguided believer at a time. In his mind, persecuting these new heretics was his duty as a Pharisee, and he pursued it with extraordinary devotion. I love the idea that God, desiring a leader and a zealot for his cause, chose the best man for the job, even though he happened to be the ultimate nemesis.

Because he was such a fearsome anti-Christian figure, he had to work hard to gain acceptance and trust once he joined the Christian ranks. The series of letters that contain Paul's life story confess the captivating odyssey of his travels, his dangerous run-ins with the Jewish establishment and the Roman government, and his tireless work to grow the early Christian Church. We also see that Paul was a people person—a devout friend, a loyal leader, and a tough-love kind of preacher. He was a man always on fire for God, who made a monumental shift in his view of who God was.

With Paul as a model, it is no wonder there are so many compelling and inspired Christian conversion testimonies to follow his. Augustine's *Confessions* was part divine query, part devotional, and part autobiography. In *Confessions,* Augustine brings us along with him in the moments leading up to his protracted conversion. Because he contemplates the inspiring conversion of St. Paul and others, Augustine is devastated by his own hesitance to follow suit and let go of his worldly pleasures and vanities. His teary lamentation of the internal battle between his two "conflicting wills," spiritual and carnal, drives him deep into an Italian garden where, after much self-flagellation, he receives a divine sign in the voice of a child chanting, "Take up and read." He interprets the chanting to be a command from God to read the Gospel. And so his conversion begins with an embrace of Scripture.

Can we not all connect with Augustine's dilemma between knowing what is right in his heart and doing it? Isn't this battle between the angel on one shoulder and the devil on the other a human condition? And doesn't it permeate all areas of our lives? I can so relate to Augustine's lamentation in the garden: his queries to himself, his friends, and God, which amount to, Why can't I do the right thing? Why is this so hard?

This is how testimonies work. When I read Augustine, I am moved by his love of God, his desire to be more Godly, and his difficulty taking the right steps over the cliff of conversion. Even after he jumps over that cliff, I connect with how he remains in touch with his human limitations ("Narrow is the mansion of my soul; enlarge Thou it, that Thou mayest enter in.") I am comforted by Augustine's honest self-reflection. If Augustine—the influential bishop, the Christian icon, and the saint—felt unsure, unclear and unworthy, perhaps it's not so unreasonable when I do, too.

Another satisfying conversion story is Herman Hesse's fictional *Siddhartha*. The story, published in 1922, is a richly woven tale that takes place in ancient India. It tells of the spiritual journey of a man who was born into a wealthy family and comes to renounce his wealth and worldly pursuits to become an ascetic. His vow of homelessness and poverty is interrupted when he encounters a beautiful courtesan who offers him lessons in the art of love. Her offer, however, is conditioned on his becoming a man of means again. So Siddhartha, in pursuit of this woman, quickly becomes a successful merchant and with the help of his courtesan, immerses himself in a life of comfort and luxury. After a time, he comes to feel empty and spiritually depleted, so much so that he decides to end his life. He goes to his favorite river to kill himself. But something happens internally for him, a spiritual shift that halts his suicide attempt and sets him back on his path to enlightenment.

Though Siddhartha is a book of fiction, it is, according to biographers, deeply reflective of the author's journey into Eastern theology. Hesse used *Siddhartha* to share the Indian philosophy and Buddhist teachings in which he had immersed himself. Donald McClory, in his *Introduction to Herman Hesse,* notes that Part One of *Siddhartha* is structured to reflect Buddha's Four Noble Truths and Part Two, his Eightfold Path. These two central tenets of Buddhism form the foundation for Hesse's twelve chapters. Hesse has said that the writing of the second half of the book was delayed because, in his own spiritual practice, he hadn't reached the "transcendental state of unity to which Siddhartha aspires." With Siddhartha, then, we can trace the author's own spiritual awakening and his pursuit of enlightenment, and we can go along for the ride, picking up the pieces and crumbs (and the big ole whole loaves) of spiritual meaning along the way.

Conversions are by no means the only type of testimony. Young Todd Burpo, Dr. Mary Neal, and others[9] have contributed to an entire genre of stories about the journey to heaven and back. Sara Maitland, in *A Book of Silence*, gives an account of her pursuit of and love affair with silence, and how it has transformed her life. And Anne Lamott has offered her short but poignant *Help, Thanks, Wow: The Three Essential Prayers,* wherein she shares what she has discovered about prayer.

If you are among the fortunate people who have experienced a spiritual awakening or a monumental religious shift, it is no wonder that you may be so imbued with inspiration that you, like so many authors before you, are seized with the desire to write. Frequently, the desire to write stems from the pressing obligation to share newly encountered lessons and spiritual truths. Otherwise, why did God choose you for this transformation, you might ask? Why were you knocked

9 Just a tiny sampling of what is available of this type of testimony:

Mary C. Neal , *To Heaven and Back: A Doctor's Extraordinary Account of Her Death, Heaven, Angels and Life Again: A True Story* (Colorado Springs: Waterbrook Press, 2012).

Todd Burpo and Lynn Vincent, *Heaven Is for Real: A Little Boy's Astounding Story of His Trip to Heaven and Back* (New York: Thomas Nelson / Harper Collins Christian Publishing, 2010).

Rita Bennett, *To Heaven and Back* (New York: Zondervan / Harper Collins Christian Publishing, 1997).

Sid Roth and Lonnie Lane, *Heaven Is Beyond Your Wildest Expectations: Ten True Stories of Experiencing Heaven* (Shippensburg, PA: Destiny Image Publishers, 2012).

Crystal McVea and Alex Tresniowski, *Waking Up in Heaven: A True Story of Brokenness, Heaven, and Life Again* (New York: Simon & Schuster, 2013).

off of your horse-of-an-ordinary-life, if not to be an example and to use your testimony to help others?

Testimonies, then, so powered by passion of a godly sort, ought to be easily written. Understandably, when the inspired sit down to write, they expect the prose to flow through them as surely happens with all spiritually inspired works. But putting spirit into words is not a task for the faint of heart. Sometimes this writing is difficult and a novice testifier may find that new words to describe the awesome beyond "awesome" are slow coming.

The best way to overcome the challenges of writing your testimony is to remember two overriding principles. The first principle is to focus on your story, not your lessons. And the second principle is to find your own voice.

FOCUSING ON THE STORY

Fresh from a profound spiritual encounter—be it a short and sweet ah-ha moment or a long tumultuous trial—the temptation is to spare your readers the moment or the trial and give them the goods, those powerful lessons learned. But the adage "show, don't tell" holds especially true for these life lessons. You may think you are being merciful by laying the lessons out in a straightforward, concise manner—like a laundry list—with bullet points and numbered paragraphs. But the best way, if you want the message to stick, is to put the laundry list of lessons aside and focus on the story behind them. Yes, the magic is in the telling of the ah-ha moment or the tumultuous trial. Mark Nepo, in *The Book of Awakening*, reflects upon the difference between lesson-telling and story-telling when he says:

It seems that the ancient medicine men understood that listening to another's story somehow gives us the strength of example to carry on, as well as showing us aspects of ourselves we can't easily see. For listening to the stories of others—not to their precautions or personal commandments—is a kind of water that breaks the fever of our isolation. If we listen closely enough, we are soothed into remembering our common name.

Scientists have found that our brains hold onto information much better when it is presented as a story. When we are given information in a presentational form, with bullet points and graphs, only the language-processing part of the brain is activated. But when we are told a story that includes movement, our motor cortex is activated. And when the story incorporates how something feels to the touch, our sensory cortex gets involved. Share a story about the deliciousness of your favorite chocolate cake and your reader's brain is activated in those parts that experience the sensations and the pleasure of eating. So when we tell and hear stories, we are putting our entire brains to work.[10]

---

10 "The Science of Storytelling: Why Telling a Story Is the Most Powerful Way to Activate Our Brains," Leo Widrich, posted 12/05/2012, available online at:
http://lifehacker.com/5965703/the-science-of-storyteling-why-telling-a-story-is-the-most-pow erful-way-to-activate-our-brains.

We are, then, especially suited to share and receive testimony stories. Princeton researchers found that the brain activity of the storyteller can synchronize with the brain activity of the listener when a story is shared. So if I am sharing a story that activates my frontal cortex (the part of the brain responsible for reason, discernment, and other higher-thinking functions), that area will light up for my listeners as well. The same is true for the emotional regions of the brain. Thus when we tell a story that has an emotional punch, we have the power in the telling to affect others in the same way, at the same time. We know this from our own experiences. I recently participated in a leadership group discussion with twenty strangers. We sat in a circle and as a way to introduce ourselves, we were asked to tell a seven-minute story. The person who went first didn't tell much about herself, but the bit she did share was emotionally captivating. Already, someone in the circle was on the verge of tears. The next person's story was even more emotionally revealing. There was more crying and shaking of heads in empathetic agreement. At this point, the group was totally engaged, mentally and emotionally engrossed in each story. After the circle session, we all expressed our amazement at the depth of our own sharing among these virtual strangers. Many said they shared much more personal information about themselves than they had originally intended. Remember, this was not a twelve-step program meeting where participants come expecting to lay open their most difficult experiences. This was a leadership forum. And yet, from the first story, the group was synchronized in their experience—so much so that they not only lived the stories of all of the others, but each was moved to share at a level much deeper than they had initially planned. It all started with the emotional and descriptive content of the first personal story.

True storytelling is too important a superpower to abandon for the sake of expediency. Your testimony may be, for you, your most significant story. It changed the course of your life, and you are pretty certain that this turning point holds life-changing lessons for others, too. And you are right. It does. So when you write your story, make sure it is *the story*. Don't cheat your readers by skipping right to the lessons. If you do, not only do you miss transferring onto them the experience that you lived in a memorable way, but you take the risk of foreclosing the additional treasures they may pick up for themselves.

One of the powers of a story is that it can take on meaning for others beyond those of the writer. As an author, one of my greatest joys is joining a book club meeting with a group that has read my book. These are joyful opportunities not simply because a group of people has decided to buy and read my book (which *is* pretty great). They are also joyful because these gatherings offer the distinct pleasure of hearing how my words have affected others. I am often amazed at the different interpretations expressed by readers. It is thrilling, humbling, and a little frightening how profoundly varied the experiences of each individual in one small group can be while processing the same information. This truth—that people experience the same book differently—is, after all, the whole point of book-club gatherings.

On a larger scale, the lucky writer sees her words spread across the globe to the nooks and crannies of the world, where through different languages and cultures people unknown to her will most assuredly interpret and utilize her information differently. This is the beauty of the written word. German author Katharina Hagena's debut work of fiction, *The Taste of Apple Seeds*, has been translated into twenty languages. She says this about her experience of writing an international bestseller her first time out:

"Every time the postman brings a box with copies of a new translation, it is a surprise party. . . . I am very moved when my book is read by people whose language I don't know or who don't know mine, who may never have entered a German kitchen and probably never will, but who might still understand more of my concerns than my neighbor next door."[11]

Even if your testimony is not translated into dozens of languages, you want it to endure and offer meaning beyond the insight that you have gleaned. Tell your story and let the story tell your lessons. In this way, you will not limit the scope or impact of your words once you release them out into the world.

Another compelling reason your testimony needs to be a story (and not a sermon) is that most people don't like to be told what to do. Even people who buy instructional books

---

11 "Guest Author Katharina Hagena on Her Debut Being Translated Into 24 Languages", Isabella Costello, posted 01/16/2013, available online at:
https://isabelcostelloliterarysofa.com/2013/01/16/guest-author-katharina-hagena-on-her-debut-being-translated-into-24-languages/.

seldom respond well to preachy prose that skips the story for the directive. I have already discussed that we humans better enjoy, learn and retain the lesson when it is couched in a story. Usually, when you offer a story, it comes with everything you need—the lesson and the why and the how of the lesson. Without it, readers revert to their three-year-old selves and spend the entire reading experience asking the nagging question: "But why?"

Good stories provide the cause and effect that our brains crave. They give us context and furnish social and emotional hooks upon which we can hang our own baggage. Without the story, we are left wondering who you are and why you think we should listen to you. Your testimony will only matter to us if your story matters—the story part is how we make the connection to what you want to impart.

FINDING YOUR OWN VOICE

And speaking of you, the writer . . .

When hungry readers are strolling down the spirituality aisles of a bookstore, searching for an uplifting, life-altering testimony to satisfy their craving for meaning, what will make them pick up, read a bit of the first chapter, and then buy *your* book?

One reason is your unique voice.

Some of my favorite authors are my favorite authors because of their distinctive voices. I imagine that I could be sitting in a pub, and it happens to be a pub where all of my favorite authors hang out. My back is to the bar and unbeknownst to me Stephen King walks up, orders a drink, and begins to chat with the bartender. I know immediately who is sitting there by how he can weave the ordinary with the truly creepy and how he uses expletives in just the right place. I know. And then there are two women sitting at an adjoining table, and they are casually chatting with each other. Without turning in their direction, I know the homey, Irish accent and the plain, direct way of Maeve Binchy. And I recognize Amy Tan's self-deprecating humor sprinkled with a heavy Chinese accent used only to drive home a point or a feeling. I know in real life I likely cannot distinguish their real voices by their words on the page, but I know their literary voices so well, I almost feel as if I can.

We writers talk incessantly about finding our voices. We aspire to an authentic one and adore writers who have achieved it. We all know these writers. They are on the bestsellers lists and their books are in the library on the classic literature display. Once you have discovered (uncovered) your own voice, you've found the holy grail of writing. Someone else said that, I cannot remember who. But it's true.

Perhaps it was Anne Lamott, who has also said (in *Bird by Bird: Some Instructions on Writing and Life)*, "We write to expose the unexposed. Most human beings are dedicated to keeping that one door shut. But the writer's job is to see what's behind it, to see the bleak unspeakable stuff, and to turn the unspeakable into words—not just into any words, but if we can, into rhythm and blues. You can't do this without discovering your own true voice . . ."

Your voice is a combination of your writing style and how your writing actually sounds in your head and when spoken out loud. In Ground Rule #1 in Chapter Two, I suggest that you start out writing the same way in which you speak. Pretend you are talking to a good friend over lunch, your spouse while the two of you are lounging in bed together, or your therapist. In other words, get your story down in the way that you would tell it to someone who cares about you and when you are at your most comfortable.

But understand that writing the same way that you speak is only a way to begin. It is a technique to help you get your first draft down. Your speaking voice is perhaps the first step in birthing your writing voice, but it is not the final step.

My best advice is to simply be aware that your writing should have a style and a feel that is your own—and to read. When we read the books of wonderful writers, we connect with the way they express their ideas—the cadence and tempo of their prose, how their phrases are turned and the style with which they string their words together. As you read other writers, try to articulate what you like about them—not with the intention to impersonate their voices, but with the goal of understanding this concept of voice. And as you work at your stories, your voice will surface. The idea is to get a grasp of what this means and then to pay attention to how your rhythm of writing sounds and feels as you go. Like your favorite authors, your voice will be what makes your writing distinctive. When you achieve your authentic voice, you will know because others will tell you. Tracy Kidder, the Pulitzer Prize–winning author, in *Good Prose: The Art of Nonfiction*, the wonderful book he's written with editor Richard Todd, advises writers in pursuit of their writing voice to: "Listen to yourself, and listen to those writers who are so great that they cannot be imitated."

The importance of reading the works of others cannot be stressed enough. And you don't have to limit your reading to nonfiction. If you are lucky to get your hands on a good book of any kind, read it. Fine writing is always worth your time. Stephen King wrote a classic book on the craft of writing, titled simply *On Writing: A Memoir of the Craft*, that is a must-read for anyone aspiring to write. In it, King repeatedly extolls the necessity of reading for good writing. He says, "Can I be blunt on this subject? If you don't have time to read, you don't have the time (or the tools) to write. Simple as that."

He drives home the point even more poignantly when he says, "You cannot hope to sweep someone else away by the force of your writing until it has been done to you."

A Testimony:
Story of a Heart

This story begins with a heart attack. So many stories end there. But this one begins. Actually, the heart attack did not actually occur. This is a story about the moment right before the heart attack—really many moments before many potential heart failures. It is about a heart that could have died, that was supposed to. But didn't.

This is a *what if* story. It is a story about the story that was supposed to happen, but mercifully went off track. And it is about what you do when you are spared.

What you do when your life is barreling down one path to what seems an inevitable end, but something simple and mundane happens that stops fate. The thing that is supposed to stop is the heart. But it doesn't.

And so what do you do with that almost thing, with finality that is thwarted?

On the eve of our thirtieth anniversary, my husband, Jon, is thinking about how fleeting life is, how fast and mercilessly it carries you along. At age fifty-one, he is thinking that he still feels like the young kid he was thirty years ago, and thus how shocking it is that he is so far down his life road, with five children, demanding businesses, and so much left to do. And as a result of these thoughts and the need of a business loan, Jon pursues more life insurance. In order to up his insurance ante, he must have a physical exam. It is this insurance-mandated physical exam that saves the life he is contemplating.

People who feel fine should not have abnormal EKGs. Their cardio stress tests should not show substantial blockage in their hearts. People who have no symptoms should not have to go into the hospital for a couple of vascular stents and end up in quintuple bypass surgery. People with only one unobstructed artery ought to know that they are a walking time bomb. But Jon had no idea.

And so the heart attack that should have happened when we raced from one terminal to the next to catch our connecting flight to London, didn't. And when Jon jogged jovially up that long stairway, keeping pace with me as I rode the escalator from London's Underground, nothing but a little breathlessness occurred. The heart attack that surely could have happened on the transatlantic flight to Europe, or on the flight coming back, or when we made vacation love in our luxury hotel after champagne and strawberries, those didn't happen either. That catastrophic heart failure that would surely have ended his life, since there was only one blood vessel still left clear, did not occur.

The point here, really, isn't about the heart attack, or the heart that just kept working despite itself. It's about second chances.

When your spouse is spared in this way (when so many people are not) you can't help but wonder why. Why him? Why us?

The brilliant surgeon, who waltzed into our lives and performed the difficult surgery as if he were simply replacing the plumbing under our kitchen sink, assured us that he would fix Jon's heart and that Jon would be a new man. While he took the hours to do that, I sat in the waiting room in deep conversation with God. It's the longest conversation God and I have had yet. Longer than the talk we had the night before the California bar exam; longer than our chat before my follow-up ultrasound after a questionable mammogram; even longer than our conversation between the amniocentesis and the obstetrician visit about the results when my last-born child was at risk. This particular God-me conversation in the heart center waiting room was not a series of negotiations, like all of the others had been. This was a conversation of gratitude. I knew that Jon had already dodged the bullet. We had the luxury of discovering his struggling heart before it cried out. We had the luxury of shopping for the right surgeon and preparing ourselves for the necessary life changes.

And so I thanked God for giving me another chance to care for Jon the way I should have all of these years. I should have been tending to his heart. It is my job as his wife to take care of the one organ that never rests. I knew that he had a family history of heart disease, and I knew his cholesterol was high. I knew that the ice cream we shared as a bedtime ritual was not good for us, and especially not him. But I didn't take heed. Most importantly, I did not make him go to the doctor every year, as a wife is supposed to do. I let him squirm his way out of basic self-maintenance, with excuses and complaints about work conflicts.

Jon's heart is what has guided him through this life. He is an acutely intelligent soul. But mostly, he navigates the world by feeling. When the doctor showed us a diagram of Jon's heart and all of the arteries through which blood could no longer travel, I couldn't help thinking of downtown Los Angeles at rush hour. We know that our diets and lifestyles must change. But in a larger sense, one must contemplate what it means when all of the routes to your city center are too blocked to get through. What is the real cause of that perpetual traffic jam?

The sudden reality, when you think you are a healthy person and you find out that you are not, is like a religious conversion. In that moment when your life changes on a dime, you get the sense that you were, just one second before, asleep—sleepwalking through your life, one foot in front of the other, tending to *important* things. You get the call, the report or the diagnosis, and you are instantly awake. You become crystal clear about what you need to change. You spring into action, because you must. But also because you've been jolted from your dream state of complacency and all of those previously "important" things fall away. The shift is so abrupt and so clear that it is both invigorating and terrifying at the same time.

Because heart disease is still the number-one killer of both men and women in our own circles, when you find out you have it, you instantly recall the people you know who have died. And you're happy to be a part of the living club, the people with a story that is still in midchapter and not at book's end. You are happy and grateful and scared and inspired.

And you hope beyond hope that yours and your lucky spouse's inspiration and gratitude stick.

What Matters Most in Chapter Five

1. Contrary to popular belief, sharing your testimony is not the same as preaching. Focus on telling the story and let the story disclose the lessons.

2. The superpower of a story is that it can offer meaning for others beyond those known to the writer.

3. Work on finding your voice by reading and writing voraciously.

CHAPTER SIX

Your Professional Journey

"The business with the best story wins."
—Forbes Magazine

WHAT TO DO WITH A PROFESSIONAL MESS OF A STORY?

During one of our recent writing workshops for entrepreneurs, a woman who looked to be in her early fifties and was in the midst of both job-searching and launching a small online business said to me, "I understand that I need to better hone my professional story. But I've had several professional lives. What about those of us who, through the years, have been all over the place professionally and don't have a neat little coherent story to offer?"

This is such a great question for a professional writing group to consider. What if you have several divergent professional stories to tell? What if they don't fit into a tidy, linear narrative that shows one clear and shining path? What if yours seems to you to be a vanilla-colored mess of a story somewhere in between?

Not everyone has a spectacularly focused career, like Connie Rice, that lends itself naturally to a drama-packed, inspirational journey-and-quest memoir like her *Power Concedes Nothing: One Woman's Quest for Social Justice in America, from the Court Room to the Kill Zones*. Rice writes a vivid account of her brilliant career as one of the nation's most influential civil rights attorneys and how she dedicated her life to social justice and bringing peace to the gang "kill zones" of Los Angeles. The stories that comprise her memoir are of a formidable woman on a mission. Though her story is expansive and multilayered, it follows a natural and consistent course, from precocious child to excellent academician to powerful advocate who even the Los Angeles Police Department came to fear and respect. Not everyone has such an awe-inspiring professional story that follows such a logical path.

And so, what do you do if you don't? Firstly, this question is great because it strikes the very core of why writing your professional story is so important an exercise. And secondly, it illustrates why the one-story-at-a-time approach can be so helpful.

In the world of business, as *Forbes* magazine puts it, "the company with the best story wins." Whether yours is a big company or a small one, your story is what draws people to you. It's what makes you relatable and connects you to others. People like to hire, do business with, and buy from people who are similar either to who they are or who they'd like to be. The early chapters of this book have already convinced you, I hope, that the most effective way to inform, inspire, teach, or motivate another person is through storytelling. I've mentioned that research shows we humans are hardwired with a preference for receiving information through stories, and thus stories are an efficient way to foster connection. In the business context, connection is the name of the game. Stories are not the *only* way to draw others to you, your company, and your product. They are just the best, most effective way. Used properly, your many professional stories, anecdotes, and yarns will make up the core of your marketing efforts. They will define your brand, separate you from the pack, and draw customers to your product.

Barbara Bradley Baekgaard, cofounder of Vera Bradley, taught me the supreme power of the story in marketing. During a women's conference, Baekgaard was the luncheon keynote speaker. In an interview format, she spoke about the modest beginnings of Vera Bradley and how she and her partner, Patricia Miller, grew the company, whose charming and feminine handbags and luggage are the cornerstones of a beloved worldwide brand. This multi-billion dollar business began with two friends at an airport, awaiting a flight. As they sat and people-watched, they noticed woman traveler after woman traveler pass by with drab and uninspired luggage. There were no attractive, feminine-looking bags anywhere in the travel landscape. So they decided right then to fill the void.

These two housewife-entrepreneurs were not new to business innovation. They'd tried their hands at other small business endeavors. But this time, with the $500 each borrowed from their husbands, they built an empire initially by sewing the distinctive high-end handbags themselves. I love that, according to Baekgaard, they started out thinking big, by approaching the larger department stores and well-known retailers to stock their handbags. I love that they filled their corporate positions with family members (and still do). I love that they adopted a pro-employee company focus and worked at creating a positive corporate culture from the beginning. I love that the company name, Vera Bradley, is Baekgaard's mother's name, and that her mother worked for the company as a sales representative well into her advanced years and until her death. When Baekgaard, who is so irreverently funny she could do stand-up comedy, said that she and her partner first considered naming one of their first businesses, a wallpaper-hanging business, "Well Hung," she won me over and turned me into a life-long admirer . . . and a devoted customer!

Before I heard her story, I was not a fan of Vera Bradley handbags. Frankly, their trademark floral patterns did not appeal to me. And their signature quiltlike fabric was not my preference for a carryall. But after Baekgaard's talk, honestly, I love the bags because I love her. I love her because I connect with her story—of homespun business acumen and chutzpah. She transformed me from ambivalent shopper to loyal customer. She literally changed the way I perceive her product. This is no small transition. Now, I buy the bags as gifts for my friends and myself because I want us to own a piece of her humor, bravery, and irreverent audacity. This is what those handbags mean to me.

Her story did that.

Now granted, Vera Bradley has a loyal international following. Their products are unique and functional, and with them, these savvy businesswomen addressed an unfilled niche. Even without Baekgaard's story, the bags sell. But the story adds a context and emotional power that transcends the bags, for women of all ages. As an attendee at the women's conference luncheon, I was among a crowd of three thousand women listening to her story. Imagine the number of new loyal customers Barbara Bradley Baekgaard won over that afternoon.

Stories sell. Stories create emotional connection. Stories cultivate loyalty. This is why tending to your professional stories carefully is so important to your business and career endeavors.

Secondly, in response to the question—how to extract coherent professional stories from a mish-mash of work experiences—I want to take a commercial break to remind you of the fundamental message of this book: your life story is comprised of many stories. You are in control of which stories you tell, and of course, how you tell them. Your professional journey is a string of stories that make up how you got to where you are now. Which of these stories you decide to tell should depend on your purpose for telling them and to whom you are telling them. The best approach for both beginner and pro is to take it one story at a time.

Valerie Khoo, Australian speaker and author of *Power Stories: The Eight Stories You Must Tell to Build an Epic Business*, suggests that there are crucial stories entrepreneurs must be prepared to tell in order to grow an "epic" business. (Who doesn't want to be epic?) These stories are the passion story, the pitch story, the business story, the customer story, the leader's story, the product story, the media story, and the personal story. Each of these stories serves a unique audience and purpose in the business-marketing landscape. In your passion story, for example, you would share what drives you and motivates you in your endeavors. The passion story has an emotional core, which is what distinguishes it from your business story. Your business story tells (hopefully compellingly) the details of what your business is, the nuts and bolts of how your business addresses particular needs and what sets it (or you) apart.

Whether you are writing your professional story for publishing or for business-marketing purposes, the number-one and number-two rules of storytelling (storytelling of any kind) have to do with audience and purpose. Rule Number One: always be mindful of your audience. And (closely related) Rule Number Two: keep your purpose in the forefront of your writing. As Khoo's *Power Stories* illustrates, these two questions—who is your audience and what is your purpose—are especially important with regard to the professional stories you choose to tell.

So how you craft an interesting and helpful professional story from the hodge-podge of your work experiences depends on to whom you want to tell your story. If you want to get your history down or write a book that features the winding and unpredictable way your career has progressed, then you can include all of your varied stories. But if you want to pinpoint your experiences to a specific job or clientele, then you will choose only the story or stories that highlight those relevant areas of your work and background.

My professional journey, for better or for worse, is a perfect example of this quandary. My career has been down one road and then another and another, waylaid by marriage and children and a shared family wanderlust. I am a lawyer by training and a writer by vocation, meaning that though I am a licensed attorney, I no longer practice law. I have been called to write, with a few other jobs held in between and concurrently, including human resources, teaching, and speaking. A person must say that she has "been called to write" when she leaves a good-paying profession, as I had, in order to pursue this not-so-good paying one. But there is more to my story, and here it is:

I practiced law for a short time in the commercial real estate group of a very large law firm. I had an exciting and promising career in a lofty skyscraper to which I took a cab each morning over and through the steep and windy streets of San Francisco. I'd had two children while in law school. Then, after passing the bar, I disappeared into the deep hole of law-firm life just as my husband quit his job as the youngest vice president of a bank to launch his own firm. Our nanny ran our children's lives and our household, which at that time was a small but charming flat in San Francisco's Pacific Heights neighborhood, surrounded by playgrounds, trendy restaurants, and other young, busy families. It was a beautiful life filled with finely tailored suits, challenging work, and sweet (but short) weekends alongside the little pond at the edge of the Presidio, feeding ducks under the gaze of the Golden Gate Bridge.

When we decided to relocate to Southern California, we moved to Malibu. I transferred to the same law firm's real estate group in Downtown Los Angeles. And so I had to transform from city-dwelling cab-catcher to beachcombing commuter. Poor me. (Of course, I spent more time commuting than beachcombing, by a long shot!) Still these were good times. And yet still, in short order, I found that the rigors of juggling a law practice, family business, and family were taking a toll on all of us. The truth is, I loved the law practice I had chosen. I loved negotiating the purchase and sale of little downtown pieces of land and putting together a ground lease that would be the foundation of some future monolithic high-rise building. I loved hashing out and then drafting a document that reflected the gainful coming together of two opposing sides of a mutual enterprise—a shopping center, business park, or golf course. I loved the rush of "closing" week, when we were finally down to the last details before happy clients exchanged deeds and keys for the chance to move on to their next big thing. I loved all of these pieces and parts of the law firm practice—the view of downtown from the thirtieth floor, lunch at my desk over a contract, the income. But I didn't love it as a mother and a wife. I didn't love scheduling travel so that I could fly out after school drop-off and return before bedtime story. I didn't love the nanny running everything except my work life, even though I knew then and would later prove that she was far better at it than I ever was. I felt that I wanted to know my husband and children again—here is the huge assumption that I knew them well in the first place. It is really only now, a couple of decades later, seasoned and scarred by this last nasty economic recession, that I can look back on those days and shake my head. The problems I perceived then, which really stemmed from wanting more than I already had, were, as my now college-aged children say, such First World problems. Then we had the luxury to contemplate that perhaps we could actually improve on such a good, solid life. And when I became pregnant with my third child, we agreed that I should leave the practice and manage the home. It is in this period of being at home, which meant leaving the structured work world of adults for the mayhem of a house full of children, that I rediscovered my *need* to write.

That is one story. Here is another.

Gina Carroll began writing, blogging, and speaking after leaving a large corporate law practice to become a stay-at-home mom to raise her five children. She is now nationally recognized for her coverage of the parenting and family landscape, including relationships, digital fluency, parenting adolescents, and getting into college. She is the author of *24 Things You Can Do with Social Media to Help Get into College*; cofounder of Inspired Wordsmith, a writing, educational and authorship services company; and cocreator of the *Tell Your Story* Workshops at AStoryThatMatters.com. She is a passionate spokesperson and blogger for MomsCleanAir Force.org and the UN Foundation's Shot@Life campaign. On her sites, Tortured by Teenagers, ThinkActParent.com, and ThinkActEat.com, Carroll also advocates for literacy, dropout prevention, and the importance of the family meal. She is a graduate of Stanford University and UCLA Law School.

The sharp contrast between these two stories illustrates the enormous landscape in which the seeds, shrubs, and trees of your professional journey are planted and rooted. The first story about my early law career and the forces that ended it would not be sent to a prospective employer. I wrote and shared that story as part of a conference discussion about work-life balance. The second story is a traditional professional biography that I use when I am a featured speaker or presenter at gatherings or publications related to writing, especially in connection with my parenting book or my work with women. If I got knocked on the head (really hard) tomorrow and decided to return to the law practice, this is not the biography I would submit to a law firm.

These stories are very different in length, tone, and focus. In both, I left out all sorts of information about the various odd jobs and professional roles I've taken on over the years. I left them out because they were not relevant to my very specific audiences. And this is what you must do: pick and choose which stories to tell and how to tell them for your specific audiences and purposes.

Even if you feel your stories are thin, with gaping holes, this may be more a sign of a misalignment of job choices than your storytelling ability. This problem is beyond the scope of this book. But with regard to the material of your life experiences, you must use whatever it is that you've got. Don't force it. And don't lie. Contrary to popular belief, writing fiction in the name of a professional story is not the way to go. In one of my many professional meanderings, I did payroll, benefits, and hiring for a few of my husband's businesses. In that role, I can tell you that I encountered more fictional work history stories than I can begin to count. Though creativity is helpful in crafting an interesting and thorough description of your skills and gifts, your creativity should not include falsehoods. Lies on your résumé, biography, or narrative can be catastrophic when the truth is uncovered.

In our family business, we once hired a gentleman for an executive position who had an impeccable résumé and a compelling story. All of his references said that he was a "really nice guy" to boot. And in his interview, this was proven to be true. He was very personable and apparently easy to work with—except he didn't know what he was doing. His work experience was a falsehood. He had, in fact, held the positions that he claimed. But his breadth of knowledge was as short as the nail on my pinky toe and so in his new company role, he was very quickly in over his head. He was "given the freedom to pursue other opportunities" inside of a month. And he only lasted that long because he was such a nice guy. So here again the Fourth Horseman of Disclosure has reared his formidable head. Before you begin to write your professional stories, I encourage you to go back to Chapter Four and reread the section about truth. Then apply what is said there with extra stringency to your professional story. I often remind my entrepreneurial clients that the Internet, in so many ways, keeps us honest. In a very real sense, the Internet is the World Wide Web of Deception because there are so many ways to start and grow a falsehood. But in business, dishonesty uncovered online can also blow up and never die down. Well, it will eventually fade away, but it may feel like forever because on the Internet, there is no place to hide.

For Business Purposes

If you need to get your professional stories down for job-search or business-promotion purposes, I suggest that you start with the *seminal three*: the narrative, the short biography, and the elevator speech. Every working person—whether you are job hunting, pursuing capital for a business, or marketing your enterprise—can greatly benefit from sorting out these three versions of his or her story.

The Long (Kitchen Sink) Narrative

The long narrative can be many things: the beginning of your professional autobiography or memoir, an archival jewel for your family, or the foundation of the marketing plan for your company. It is your fully developed story, which may include relevant family and educational background information. In it, you should flesh out all of the experiences and people who fed, influenced, and formed your professional or vocational decisions. Your long narrative should also include all of your diversions and detours, how they happened and why. Don't forget to include the personal and emotional components of your story. These will be important even for your job or business marketing. The personal aspects of your stories are very effective hooks.

In his book, *Enchantment: The Art of Changing Hearts, Minds, and Actions,* Guy Kawasaki, charismatic and highly successful Silicon Valley entrepreneur-evangelist, writes,

"Personal stories are powerful ways to make important events real and emotional to people." And in his other book *The Art of the Start*, he says that "getting personal," meaning sharing the parts of your story that are unique revelations to you, is more effective than telling stories that are general or involve large groups of people. Kawasaki asserts that, according to research, the individual story is more compelling to people than the collective and that people have an easier time connecting to an individual occurrence than a massive one. In business, community work, or personal advancement, Kawasaki says, the personal aspects of your story that resonate with others, and that reach them emotionally, matter more than generalities and disconnected technical information.

The very purpose of the long narrative is to get all aspects of your professional endeavors down in story form. Because the two shorter versions of your story can be drawn from your long narrative, I recommend that you complete the long narrative first. This way, you will have gathered and articulated all of the material you will need for the biography and the elevator speech (or speeches). And depending on your audience and purpose, you can pick and choose from the cornucopia of experiences contained in your long narrative.

THE BIOGRAPHY

The biography is a shorter description of who you are and what you have done. It is concise and very business-focused, but it includes enough of your journey to make you interesting and three-dimensional. This is an important promotional story that focuses on your accomplishments and experiences, but it is a more detail-enriched description than a résumé, utilizing full-sentence descriptions in a story format instead of in an outline format. When you are ready to produce a biography, pull out what you need for your particular purposes from the kitchen-sink narrative. It should all be there. If you are invited to join a prestigious board of directors, your biography may be a very formal introduction of who you are. Or when you plan to speak to your local Rotary Club, they may request a more relaxed bio. Once you pull what you need, you will begin to edit.

THE ELEVATOR SPEECH

The elevator speech is your thirty-second spiel about who you are. The basis of this short introduction is this: imagine you are on your way to a job interview or a meeting with a venture capitalist or client. As you ride up on the elevator, you notice that the person you are going to meet is standing right in the elevator with you. She recognizes you also and says, "You are my next appointment, aren't you?" and you say "Yes." The two of you offer pleasantries, and then she says, "So what's this meeting about?"

You know that she knows what your meeting is about, but she asks because she is busy and she wants to decide how much time to allot to you—will she tell her secretary on her way into her office to block out more time for you or less time? Will she decide to take the interview or hand you off to some junior person who is not a decision-maker? This depends on how you respond to her question—what is this meeting about (really, what are YOU about)? You have the short ride in the elevator to convince her that you are worth her time and consideration. This is a crucial opportunity in which you can either shine or crash and burn. You must be ready with a short, confident hook of an introduction that effectively says who you are and why you are valuable to her. Many people focus on their elevator speech before they've really clarified for themselves what their professional value and values are. There are few things more painful to witness than the delivery of a poorly conceived elevator speech, the kind that does more harm than good. If you've done the work on your narrative and biography, you will have sorted out who you are, why you are unique, and what you (or your business) seek to accomplish. This is the fertile soil from which great elevator speeches emerge. Though the elevator speech is *very* short, the long narrative can help you get a handle on your overarching themes and strengths. The short biography will help you with condensed wording.

In order to keep to the thirty-second rule for your elevator speech, whittle it down to thirty-five words or less. If you keep it to thirty-five or less, then when you need to, you have a little room to change it to suit the venture capitalist in the elevator, the major funder at your gala table, *and* the CEO at the cocktail party. Once you get your elevator speech written and edited, memorize it. This is a story that you must be ready to share at any given moment when opportunity arises. And lastly, remember, the elevator speech is designed to hook the big catch. And so you must leave your audience with the feeling that they *need* to hear what you have to offer.

Your elevator speech should end with a hook that motivates your audience to say, "Tell me more!"

To summarize the process I am suggesting for your professional stories: write your long narrative first, followed by your biography, and then your elevator speech. These three basic stories will serve you well for your many purposes and allow you to easily pull from and repurpose your material for the other business stories, like the eight important stories that Khoo suggests, as your business and publishing needs require.

THE EDITOR WITHIN

"So the writer who breeds more words than he needs, is making a chore of the reader who reads."

—Dr. Seuss

Editing is the process by which you make your story as clean and simple as possible. This is no easy task. It is, however, a deeply satisfying one. When Mark Twain made his now-famous apology in his correspondence to a friend, "I didn't have time to write a short letter, so I wrote a long one instead," he is getting at the crux of the editing challenge. The exercise of putting your story in its cleanest, shortest form is a craft that takes time and effort.

And because editing can be time-consuming work—A. J. Liebling said, "I can write better than anybody who can write faster, and I can write faster than anybody who can write better"—you should consider it a gift to your reader and yourself, this toiling to make your sentences as pristine as possible. When you take the time to read again what you have written and to wrangle with the words to make them more clearly express your thoughts, your story becomes more true to itself. Editing should bring you closer to your authentic voice and intent, not further afield. And so I recommend that you let go of any notions that your first thoughts are your purest. This is a belief that is commonly held but far from the truth.

For the last session of a group leadership seminar that I participated in with a group of colleagues, we were asked to give a summary of our experiences together. About one third of us spoke from a written response that had been prepared before this final meeting, and others spoke without any prepared notes. Among those without a prepared statement, several said before they spoke, "I've decided to speak from the heart today," or "I'm just speaking from the heart here . . ." After maybe the fifth person said something about speaking from the heart, some of us with prepared statements began to roll our eyes in mild annoyance. How is it, we prepared folk wondered, that expressing your feelings without forethought and planning better represents "speaking from the heart"?

I find the opposite to be true. When you have much to say and you want to guarantee that you have covered it all in the limited time allotted, you are best served by preparation. You must get all of your thoughts down and then you must go through your ideas to make them succinct and poignant. This is hard to do off-the-cuff and in the moment. Granted, some people can speak very well spontaneously. But I would argue that even those well-spoken specimens would make a better statement if they'd prepared first. A prepared statement on which time has been spent, that has been pondered and then refined to its most meaningful and effective format, is most surely a gift from the heart. It is no less sincere. Arguably, it is more so, for the sacrifice and devotion paid to it.

And this is how we must approach all editing. Even though the words of your first draft are vitally important, and even though you must let them flow without hindrance, your *best* version will take form as you edit. Like a phoenix rising out of the ashes, your final copy will be a wholly different animal than your first draft, if you are willing to put in the time. And you must.

As S. Kelley Harrell, author and neoshaman, says, "Editing is the very edge of your knowledge forced to grow—a test you can't cheat on." Your own self-editing is the process of looking over your words again and again, until you have coerced them into the highest expression of your thought. Hopefully, this does not cause you to push away from your computer or drop your feathered quill pen and walk away. Instead, embrace this part of the process. Like Toni Morrison, fall in love with the idea of revising and crafting your work. She says:

The best part of it all, the absolutely most delicious part, is finishing it and then doing it over. That's the thrill of a lifetime for me: if I can just get done with the first phase and then have infinite time to fix it and change it.

If you cannot channel Toni Morrison, then think of yourself as the sculptor Michelangelo. Your first draft is your slab of clay or stone. And you are going to chip and shape away, until your masterpiece is complete.

RECOMMENDATIONS FOR REVISING YOUR DRAFT(S)

Once you have completed your first draft:

Read Again.

Read your story again. Make changes and improvements. You may feel that you need to fill in some details or flesh out facts. Don Roff says, "I've found the best way to revise your own work is to pretend that somebody else wrote it and then to rip the living sh*t out of it." You don't have to be so violent with your hard-wrought treasure . . . unless you need to be. If you pretend that your work is someone else's, you may be better able to separate from your ego and from your attachment to passages that initially felt brilliant when you first wrote them but no longer really have a place. Or you may find an even more brilliant way to state them. Roff is right in his assessment that you must be ruthless.

WWWWW&H Check.

There are questions every good writer answers. If they are not addressed, you've left a hole that will likely distract and/ or disappoint your readers. So check your writing and make sure you fill the holes:

WHO: Who are the characters? Have you fleshed out who they are and why they are important to the story?

WHAT: What is the focus or theme of your story?

WHEN: When did your story occur—when in history? How old were you?

WHERE: Where does the story take place—the city? What space does it inhabit (your kitchen, your school, etc.)?

WHY: Why is it important? Why should we care?

HOW: How did you get here—into the world (birth), in your predicament, or at this professional crossroad?

Walk Away.

Walk away from the story. Take a break of at least a full day, where you do not read or contemplate the story during the break. And only then return, refreshed and ready to look upon your work with new eyes and new energy!

Active Voice.

As you read through a second time, look for passive sentences and change them to the active voice. In other words, try to use sentences that are succinct and engage an action verb. Passive sentences tend to be longer, less interesting, and make the reader work harder for meaning. So for example, you might replace "The cake was baked this afternoon" with "I baked the cake this afternoon." Patricia T. O'Conner, in her book *Words Fail Me,* calls the passive voice "anemic writing." O'Conner says people often write passively when they want to obscure blame. Her example is: "Mistakes were made." When written in this way, nobody is at fault for the mistakes. This sentence is weak and cowardly. Instead, be brave, go ahead and admit guilt: "I made mistakes." Your reader will appreciate your strength and your commitment to clarity.

Technical Writing Assistance.

For English usage, style, and proper citation, refer to the *Chicago Manual of Style,* long considered the authority on the writing and citation styles widely used in publishing. And even though you have the spell-check function on your computer, the *Merriam-Webster Dictionary* is the industry standard for the latest proper spellings. Don't guess if you are unsure about usage. Look it up. You can find the *Chicago Manual of Style, Merriam-Webster* and all other manner of help online (http://www.chicagomanualofstyle.org and https://www.merriam-webster.com). If you choose resources other than the *CMS or Merriam-Webster,* just make sure your sources are reliable.

Seek New Eyes.

When you feel that your story is complete, ask one (or a few) honest and well-meaning people to read it and give you feedback. Use the feedback that you feel is helpful, and throw out the rest.

When to Stop.

Sometimes, those of us who lean toward perfectionism do not know when to stop editing. And since a work can always be improved, you will likely never reach that moment when, as you read your work, a bell goes off in your head and you know you are done.

Antoine de Saint-Exupéry, French aviator and writer, said:

> *"Perfection is finally attained not when there is no longer anything to add but when there is no longer anything to take away, when a body has been stripped down to its nakedness."*

This notion of completion is the same as Dr. Seuss's admonishment about the writer who breeds more words than she needs. So as a measure to help you know when your work is complete, consider this test: once your story is (1) cleared of as many extraneous and unnecessary words as possible so that it is bare in clarity and truth, (2) pleasing to you, in form and substance, and (3) suitable for your purposes, you are finished.

Here is another measure: if you get to a point where you cannot bear to look at the blasted thing one more time, chances are it still needs work. Get some new eyes to help you. Take a break from it. And then, keep at it. When, on the other hand, you get to the point where you keep reading your story over and over again for your own enjoyment, even after you've read it a million times in the "fixing" process, then you likely have a work you are happy with. Now you are finished. Congratulations!

A Professional Passion Story: My One Thing

She wrote to me. She left her comment on my website. She told me what I'd written changed her life. She told me that I made her weep tears of relief and joy. She said she wept and then she got up and she made a change. Someone—a stranger—said that I understood her. My story was her story.

I was simply writing my own experiences. I was simply writing the truth—about motherhood, about justice, about my own need for action. I wasn't trying to make a difference—then. In the beginning, I just wanted to write. And so I wrote and I released my writings, like little clumsy Japanese water lanterns, launched at water's edge, floating away, but somehow aggregating far off in the middle of the lake, like little offerings of uncertain purpose.

For months I did this, writing, releasing, writing, releasing. But then she wrote me through her tears—an agonized mother from somewhere else—Sweden, of all places. And she told me that my words, my words, changed her life. Little did she know that in that moment of her reaching out, she also changed mine. . . .

I am a writer.

I'm a mother, a wife, a lawyer, and a teacher. But writing is what makes me bound out of bed in the morning. This wasn't always true. Good writing is hard, laborious, and solitary. To stay the course of an effort with words, to get it right—wrangling prose, coercing it to say exactly what you want it to—these are not easy things to do. As some tortured writer once said, "A blank page is God's way of showing how hard it is to be God."

But the moment I learned that this compulsion of mine to give thought and truth legs to stand on and lace-up boots to walk with, as soon as I came to understand the power of the written word to change a mind, to spur an action, to console a heavy heart, to right a wrong, to ease a pain, to shift a perspective, to start a fire and to put one out, my true life's purpose began.

In the movie *City Slickers*, when Billy Crystal's character asks Curly, the burly cowboy played by Jack Palance, how Curly had come to live so long and so self-satisfactorily, Curly says, "One Thing. One Thing." In essence, pick your one thing and do it well.

Writing. Writing for change is my one thing.

What Matters Most in Chapter Six

1. Don't think of your story as messy and unfocused. Think of it as diverse and brimming over with story potential.

2. Write your professional stories with a specific audience and purpose in mind.

3. Be truthful. (Bears repeating!)

4. Your editing goal: to wrangle with your words until your story is its cleanest, shortest, most accurate of purpose.

5. Your editing is complete when your story is:

    a. Bare in clarity and truth;

    b. Pleasing to you; and

    c. Suitable for your purpose(s).

CHAPTER SEVEN

A Word About Preparation
and Prompts

HABIT AND RITUAL

One of the challenges of writing is creating the time and space to do it. Writing is an art. In order to bring forth your best life stories in their highest form, you must treat your writing as a creative process and think of yourself as an artist.

The creation of art requires regular practice. The only way you will complete your life stories is to keep at it. The best way to keep at it is to tailor a writing habit to your life and your goals. And the best writing habits include rituals and behaviors that inspire you and keep you on track.

For our purposes, rituals and habits are not interchangeable terms. A habit is something that you do with enough regularity that it becomes automatic, so automatic and engrained that it is difficult to relinquish. A ritual is a ceremonial action performed according to a prescribed order. Rituals usually announce or signify an important occurrence. If you endeavor to create a writing routine that contains both regularity and ceremony, if you develop helpful habits that include ritual, you greatly improve your odds of success.

In *Daily Rituals: How Artists Work,* Mason Currey provides a peek into the writing rituals and habits of one hundred and sixty-one well-known artists, including a fair number of authors. The accounts in *Daily Rituals* are mostly the artists' own words. And the words of these prolific creators do more than just hint at how important is the deliberate carving out of a daily practice. They share their very personal approaches to establishing specific writing spaces and determining their optimally creative (or simply the most opportune) times to write.

Japanese author Haruki Murakami maintains a strict routine when he is working on a novel. He wakes at 4:00 a.m.; writes for five to six straight hours; spends the afternoon running errands, reading and listening to music; then goes to bed at 9:00 p.m. He does this without variation because he believes the repetition is important to keeping his mind focused and in a deeper state of consciousness.

Maya Angelou preferred to work away from home, so she kept a modest hotel room near her house where she would write from early morning to early afternoon. She found more success in the sterile setting of "a tiny, mean" hotel room furnished only with a bed and sometimes a face basin.

For her first novel, *Interview with the Vampire,* Anne Rice chose to write at night and sleep during the day. She claims the solitude and quiet of the evening hours helped her concentrate and think best. But I suspect something about that schedule was most fitting for her subject matter.

Toni Morrison developed an early morning practice by rising around 5:00 a.m., making coffee and then watching the sun rise. She says that seeing "the light come" is crucial to her routine because it is her way of approaching the mysterious process of writing. For Morrison, rising early and making coffee is part of her habit. Watching the light come is the ritual.

What most of the authors who are featured in *Daily Rituals* have in common is that they endeavor to write at the same time every day, limiting their sessions to one or two locations. As you work on your life stories, I recommend this for you, too. Spend a week testing different locations and different times of the day to determine what works best for you. When and where do you feel most productive—focused and creative?

Research shows that early morning is optimal for creative pursuits.[12] Many authors seize the a.m. hours to do their best writing. Even late-night, hard-drinking authors like Ernest Hemingway and William Faulkner managed to make the most of a regular early morning practice. Anne Rice, post-*Vampire,* eventually discovered that mornings worked

---

12 *The Best Time to Write and Get Ideas, According to Science,* Kevan Lee, posted 05/10/2014, available online at:
https://blog.bufferapp.com/the-best-time-to-write-and-get-ideas?
utm_source=rss&utm_medium=rss&utm_campaign=the-best-time-to-write-and-get
-ideas

best for her, as well. Aine Greaney, in her book, *Writer with a Day Job: Inspiration & Exercises to Help You Craft a Writing Life Alongside Your Career,* suggests another theory to explain the superiority of a morning practice. The early morning writer can capitalize on the dream state from which she has just emerged, since creative writing, according to Greaney, draws on the same subconscious side of the brain as night dreams. I like writing and researching in the morning because my family is still asleep, even the dog; the house is quiet and so is my cell phone. The stresses of the previous day are a faded memory. The key to mornings, for me, is to avoid television, emails and social media. As soon as I check my emails, the magic of the morning is over. My "day job" has officially begun.

Though most of the writers featured in *Daily Rituals* expressed a preference for solitude, their choice locations varied widely. Like Maya Angelou, I prefer to write in closed-in, austere places where I receive very little outside interference or distraction. This has meant different locations over time. Early on, I converted a walk-in closet into my writing space and found sitting in that tiny, unadorned room with no windows, just a desk, chair, lamp and laptop, very comforting for work. One of my clients loves to write in the same spot by the lake near her home. She prefers the expansiveness of the water and sky. Mark Twain locked himself in his office for the entire day, while Jane Austen wrote in the family sitting room in the company of her mother and sister, who quietly sewed nearby. When you establish the ideal creative spot for yourself, each time you arrive in that space to write, you will be able to find your focus and concentration with greater ease, as your regular location will signal to your brain that it's time to work.

Rituals help us train the brain, too, by elevating the importance of the practice with ceremony and repetition. Your ritual need not have a practical purpose outside of this. It can be any action that has meaning for you. The key is to perform it every time you begin your writing session. While she lived in France, Gertrude Stein preferred to write outdoors and liked to look at rocks and cows at intervals as she wrote. So she and her long-time companion, Alice B. Toklas, would hop into their Ford and take a drive in the country until they found a good spot. While Stein prepared herself for writing with campstool, pencil and pad, Ms. Toklas took a switch to the backside of the nearest cow to coax it into Stein's line of vision. Once inspired, Stein would only write for fifteen minutes to half-hour per session.[13] Apparently, the self-proclaimed genius spent more time engaged in the ritual than the writing. Your ritual can be as simple as lighting a candle at the beginning of your session to help mark the beginning of your writing experience, or like Toni Morrison, simply watching the sky fill with light at first dawn. Even simple actions, when done reverently and repeatedly, signal your brain that you are about to do something important. You can also add three big yawns before you begin. Researchers believe that yawning increases blood flow to the brain and promotes brain growth and activity. In this way, you equip your mind for the work ahead.

---

13 Mason Currey, *Daily Ritual: How Artists Work* (New York: Alfred A. Knopf: First Edition, 2013), 50.

So much is written about writing habit and ritual because the challenge is real, and increasingly so with our multiple electronic devices and the current twenty-four-hour information onslaught. Every moment you pay to setting up your writing habit will be well worth the effort.

A Magic Box

The Magic Box System is another habit that I strongly encourage. The process of focusing on one story necessitates the storage of ideas for later use. As you go through your exercise of fleshing out your story, you need to create a way to store the brilliant ideas and important memories that do not belong in the story you are currently composing, but deserve subsequent development. For this, I recommend a "magic box." Remember the recipe boxes you (or your mother) kept in the kitchen before the computer took over our lives? You can create a similar receptacle for your story ideas. This notion of a physical idea box is old school but effective. The magic box should contain blank index cards and index tabs just like the recipe box. You will need five tabs labeled as follows—settings, characters, scenes, dialog and themes.

As you are writing and researching, when you remember a character, like your quirky Uncle Pete, or the early version of your Grandmother before she retired, you write down the memory on an index card and deposit it in the box behind the "character" tab, and so on. If you are in the middle of writing, you may not want to file your idea cards behind the proper tab in that moment. This can wait until later.

Keeping a record of your thoughts by this simple method helps you to maintain your focus on the current story and allows you to calm your fears about getting all of your thoughts, memories and additional stories safely preserved before you lose them. And by writing them down, you get them out of your head, thereby clearing the way for work on the story at hand. The magic box also relieves you of the pressure of trying to fit all of your beautiful and important ideas, story lines and memories into one story because you fear you may lose them if you don't.

You can, of course, create a virtual version of the magic box. But the real version has advantages for the busy writer with a head full of stories and ideas. In order to record an idea in another file on your computer, you would have to leave your writing screen to do it, which can be disruptive. With the box at your side, you can jot down the thought, deposit it and then immediately return to your writing screen. The magic box also becomes a resource. If you encounter a writing block or a place where you have a gap in your story, you can go through the cards that you have accumulated to help jog your memory and prompt other ideas that might be relevant to the story you are working on. This is where the written cards are helpful. Shuffling the cards by putting them together—different settings with different characters and scenes—is a creative exercise that you cannot do as effectively if you are just using a notepad or computer files.

So I encourage you to at least start with a physical magic box. With every writing session, keep blank index cards at the ready. Your magic box is where you will go when you complete your first story and are ready to move on to the next.

Prompts by Theme

In the sections that follow, I offer a process of progressive prompts. These are not the typical prompts used for writing practice. We are not endeavoring to practice here. As You-Tube sensation and cultural icon Sweet Brown says, "Ain't nobody got time for that!"

We want to begin in the best way possible, and that is, with one story at a time. In furtherance of this, the following prompts are to help you narrow your focus, mine your memory and keep to the material that will drive your story forward. These are only suggested if you cannot start, if your mind is fuzzy on the story and/or your reason for telling it. If you are already clear about what you want to write and how you will begin, then skip the prompts altogether. You do not need them. The sections are grouped by subject matter and each section stands alone. So, depending on the type of story you intend to write (mother story, childhood, relationship, etc.), you should go directly to that section and follow the steps therein.

Remember, before you begin writing, your story idea should be clear in your head in two ways. You should be able to answer the questions:

1. What is my story about? (What theme or themes am I exploring?)

2. How do I plan to illustrate the theme or themes? (What pictures will I draw with words to bring my points to life?)

Your goal is to complete a rough draft with your ground rules in mind. And once the rough draft of your story is complete, go to Chapter Six and follow the instructions for editing your work.

THE MOTHER STORY

When preparing to write about your mother, take these steps:

1. Free-Fall Words

Think of your mother. Fill your head with her image or essence: your memory of how she smelled, spoke, and stood in your presence. Then write every word that surfaces as soon as it comes to you, even if it seems nonsensical.

2. Haunting Memories

Write any memories that continue to come to mind for you: a recurring dream or thought of your mother that remains near your mind's surface. It doesn't really need to be "haunting," just recurring. Then write about how the memory makes you feel, what effect it has on you. Why do you believe it sticks with you and remains near the surface?

3. Events

List events, scenes, interactions, and/or conversations that you remember with your mother. Record the details—any bits of memory, even if disjointed.

4. Look at the list of theme words and phrases below:

Write down any that jump out at you as applying to your mother and your relationship with your mother. (If you do not find any fitting theme words on this list, go to the other subject matter sections and try those, especially the Childhood Story and Relationship Story sections.)

Abandonment	Jealousy	Saint
Role Reversal	Role Model	Giver
Her Substance	Beauty	Parasite
Abuse	Wisdom	Smother
My substance	Teacher	Freedom
abuse	Protector	
Celebrity	Bitch	

Now let the word or phrase fill your head along with the image of your mother. Connect to this phrase or word all applicable free-fall words, haunting memories, and events that you have already listed.

5. *Write!*

Have you hooked a story or a piece of a story yet? If so, start writing. With your story ideas in mind, return to the Ground Rules in Chapter 2 and get your first draft down. If you haven't hooked a story yet, then keep mining the free-fall words, your haunting memories and events for connections to one or more of the themes you chose. You are bound to connect with an idea for a story that is meaningful to you.

6. *Remember:*

You are only writing one story at a time. If ideas, memories, or facts relating to other stories come up, write them down and deposit them in your magic box.

THE CHILDHOOD STORY

When preparing to write about your childhood, take these steps:

1. *Free-Fall Words*

Think of your childhood self. Let her or his image or essence fill your head. Then write every word that surfaces as soon as it surfaces, even if it seems nonsensical.

2. *Haunting Memories*

Write any memories that continue to come to mind about your childhood: a recurring dream or thought that remains near the surface of your mind. It does not have to be "haunting," just recurring. Then write about how the memory makes you feel, what effect it has on you. Why do you believe this memory sticks with you and stays on the surface?

3. Events

List events, scenes, interactions, and/or conversations that you remember from childhood that are related to your primary theme(s). Record the details—any bits of memory, even if disjointed.

4. Look at the list of theme words and phrases below:

Write down any that jump out at you as applying to your childhood self or your childhood in general. (If you do not find any fitting theme words on this list, go to the other subject matter sections and try those, especially the Mother Story and Relationship Story sections.)

Coming of Age	Illness/Disease	Happiness
Hardship	(your own or	Completion
Abandonment	another's)	Sisterhood
Belonging	Disability	Bond
Exclusion	Loneliness	Abuse
Bully	Euphoria	Friendship
Sustaining Power	Pride	Victory
of Love	Sibling	Accomplishment
Affection	Rivalry	Effort
	Jealousy	

Now let the word or phrase fill your head along with the image of your childhood self. Connect to this phrase or word all applicable free-fall words, haunting memories, and events that you have already listed.

5. *Write!*

Have you hooked a story or a piece of a story yet? If so, begin writing. If not, then keep mining your free-fall words and your haunting memories for connections to one or more of the themes you chose. You are bound to connect with an idea for a story that is meaningful to you. With your story ideas in mind, return to the Ground Rules in Chapter Two and get your first draft down.

6. *Remember:*

You are only writing one story at a time. If ideas, memories, or facts relating to other stories come up, write down and deposit them in your magic box.

THE RELATIONSHIP STORY

This section provides steps to take when preparing to write about any type of relationship. This could include a romantic love, a parent-child or sibling relationship or a friendship. These prompts assume that you already know about whom or what relationship you desire to write, and help flesh out which story to tell about that relationship.

1. Free-Fall Words

Think of the person, let his or her image or essence fill your head. Then write every word that surfaces as soon as it surfaces, even if it seems nonsensical.

2. Haunting Memories

Write any memories that continue to come to mind for you about this person and your relationship with him or her: a recurring dream or thought that remains near the surface. It does not have to be heavy or even deep, just recurring. Then write about how the memory makes you feel, what effect it has on you.

3. Events

List events, scenes, interactions, and/or conversations that you remember about the person or the relationship. Record the details—any bits of memory, even if disjointed.

4. Look at the list of theme words and phrases below:

Write down any that jump out at you as applying to the relationship you are writing about. (If you do not find any fitting theme words in this list, go to the other subject matter sections and try those, especially the Mother Story and Childhood Story sections.)

Power of	Rescuer	Secret
Infatuation	Friendship	Secretive
Sustaining	Divorce	Dishonesty
Power of	Date from Hell	Trust
Love	Blind Date	Confidence
Parenthood	First Meeting	Sex
(Trials,	Breakup	Unique
Rewards)	Loyalty	Cheater
Abuse	Betrayal	Fixer

Now let the word or phrase fill your head along with the image of the person you are writing about. Connect to this phrase or word all applicable free-fall words, haunting memories, and events that you have already listed.

5. Hooking a Story

Have you hooked a story or a piece of a story yet? If so, go on to step 6 below. If not, then keep mining your free-fall words and your haunting memories for connections to one or more of the themes you chose. You are bound to connect with an idea for a story meaningful to you.

6. Begin Writing Your Story

With your story ideas in mind, return to the Ground Rules in Chapter Two and get your first draft down.

7. *Remember:*

You are only writing one story at a time. If ideas, memories, or facts relating to other stories come up, write down and deposit them in your magic box.

THE TESTIMONY

You are likely very clear about the testimony you'd like to share. But you may be stumped about how to start, what to include, and how to show, not tell. In order to fine tune your story topic, you can use this process suggested for uncovering the stories you want to tell.

1. *First-Word Free Fall*

Think of the experience that you want to share. Focusing on your ah-ha moment, let the climactic part of the experience fill your head. Then write every word that surfaces as soon as it comes to you, even if it seems nonsensical or disjointed.

2. *Haunting Memories*

Write any memories that continue to come to mind about your experience—a recurring thought, or feeling that remains near the surface. It does not have to be heavy or even deep, just recurring. Then write about what effect the memory has on you (e.g., the look on the surgeon's face the moment he came out of my husband's surgery).

3. Events

List events, scenes, interactions, and/or conversations that you remember as key to the experience. Record the details—any bits of memory, even if disjointed.

4. Look at the list of theme words and phrases below:

Write down any that jump out at you as applying to your experience.

Awakening (Near Death, Near Divorce)
Conversion
Rescue/ Deliverance
Exercise of Faith (Stepping Out)
God's Call to Ministry
Turning Point
Transformative Service to Another

5. Hooking a Story

Decide which of the theme phrases that you wrote down will be your central theme and then connect your free-fall words, haunting memories, and experiences that you associated with that theme word or phrase.

6. Begin Writing Your Story

With your story ideas in mind, return to the Ground Rules in Chapter Two and get your first draft down.

7. *Remember:*

You are only writing one story at a time. If ideas, memories, or facts relating to other stories come up, write down and deposit them in your magic box.

SHARING YOUR HARD WORK

Once you have completed your story, I encourage you to share it with others. Remember that your stories are a part of your family's legacy, your gift to someone in need, and part of the fabric of human history! So step out there and share it. I also welcome an opportunity to read your work. If you are inclined, please send your final version, preferably in PDF form, to gina@inspiredwordsmith.com.

WHAT MATTERS MOST IN CHAPTER SEVEN

1. Write every day. Develop a writing habit that suits you well.

2. Make sure your writing habit includes a meaningful ritual or two.

3. Use the Magic Box System for that stream of ideas that doesn't directly relate to the story you are currently writing.

4. Only use the prompts if your story theme and illustrations are not clear enough in your head to begin.

5. When you finish your first draft, celebrate! Then go to Chapter Six and begin editing.

6. When you finish your final draft, share your story with the world!

APPENDIX:

Memoirs Worth a Read

CHILDHOOD MEMOIRS

Sober Stick Figure: A Memoir by Amber Tozer (Running Press, 2016). *Sober Stick Figure* is an addiction-and-recovery story from stand-up comedian Amber Tozer. She starts out early in life within a family tradition of alcoholism. Tales of tragedy and triumph told with tenderness and grit, seriousness and hilarity.

Between the World and Me by Ta-Nehisi Coates (Spiegel & Grau, 2015). Poetic and searing. A must read if you are willing to have your heart pierced!

A California Childhood by James Franco (Insight Editions, 2014). Actor, director, screenwriter James Franco's Northern California childhood and adolescence.

Coming Clean: A Memoir by Kimberly Rae Miller (New Harvest, 2013). Miller tells of her coming-of-age in a household filled to the brim with stuff as a result of her parents' struggle with a hoarding disorder.

Still Points North: One Alaskan Childhood, One Grown-up World, One Long Journey Home by Leigh Newman (Dial Press, 2013). Newman explores the splaying of her family in divorce, wherein she must divide her life between Baltimore with her mother and the Alaskan wild with her father.

Why Be Happy When You Could Be Normal? by Jeanette Winterson (Grove Press, 2013). "*Why Be Happy When You Could Be Normal?* is raucous. It hums with a dark refulgence from its first pages. . . . Singular and electric . . . [Winterson's] life with her adoptive parents was often appalling, but it made her the writer she is."—*The New York Times*

The Girl Nobody Wants: A Shocking True Story of Child Abuse in Ireland by Lily O'Brien (Troubador Publishing, 2012). It's one thing to be abused in the name of love. It's quite another to be abused by people who, all the while, let you know that they do not love nor want you. This is the story of childhood abuse, both sexual and emotional, written by a woman who is still living daily with the pain, trauma, and hopelessness of her devastating past.

Dragonfly: A Childhood Memoir by W. Nikola-Lisa (Gyro-Scope Books, 2010). Prolific children's book author W. Nikola-Lisa offers his insight into his childhood while growing up in a small South Texas town.

A Long Way Gone: Memoirs of a Boy Soldier by Ishmael Beah (Sarah Crichton Books, 2008). *A Long Way Gone* is a riveting first-person account of how a gentle thirteen-year-old boy is transformed into a killing machine for his government's army. As a twenty-five-year-old survivor, Ishmael Beah shares how young boys like himself are chosen, drugged, and trained to do the unimaginable. And he shares the circumstances of his own survival.

Born in the Big Rains: A Memoir of Somalia and Survival by Fadumo Korn with Sabine Eichhorst (The Feminist Press at

CUNY, 2008). Tough to read in parts, but beautifully written. This is the story of how Fadumo Korn, born among a nomadic people of Somalia, survives her own brutal and nearly fatal circumcision and escapes the political upheaval of civil war to become the anti-female-genital-mutilation activist that she is today. "A brutally honest, politically sensitive, and bold addition to literature on global women's health." — *Publishers Weekly*

An American Childhood by Annie Dillard (Harper & Row, 2008). Pulitzer Prize–winning author Annie Dillard's poignant and vivid memoir of growing up in 1950s Pittsburgh.

Blue Skies, No Fences: A Memoir of Childhood and Family by Lynne V. Cheney (Pocket Books, 2007). Lynne Cheney, former Second Lady, recreates the idyllic world of post-WWII small-town Casper, Wyoming, when and where "the country seemed in control of its destiny and individual Americans in charge of theirs." *Blue Skies* is one of those memoirs that help fill in the personal gaps we crave to know about how powerful and controversial people become who they are.

Persepolis 2: The Story of a Return by Marjane Satrapi (Pantheon, 2005). Told in comic-strip images, Marjane Satrapi's memoir is about growing up in Iran during the Islamic Revolution. This is a continuation of a story about coming-of-age during a complex and dangerous time in history amid war. *Persepolis: The Story of a Childhood* was Satrapi's triumphant first story about her beginnings. And now, with *Persepolis 2,* we get the rest of the story—what happens to our heroine into adolescence and beyond. I strongly suggest that you read them both.

Sickened: The Memoir of a Munchausen by Proxy Childhood by Julie Gregory and Marc D. Feldman, MD (Bantam, 2003). Munchausen syndrome by proxy is a disorder in which a person (usually a mother) purposely causes another person (usually her child) to become ill, in order to satisfy a need to be a caregiver. Julie Gregory was just that child, who spent much of her childhood being examined, x-rayed, medicated, and operated on at her mother's behest. Her story is a gripping and alarming tale of the little-known form of child abuse from which Gregory survives and from which she endeavors to save others.

A Girl Named Zippy by Haven Kimmel (Broadway Books, 2002). Through the voice of her child-self, Kimmel tells the story of her childhood and how she navigates her world of adults and life in the interesting times of 1965. This book is so endearing and such fun to read. Without giving anything away, I love the ending the very most.

Cherry by Mary Karr (Penguin Books, 2001). How can you put down a adolescent memoir that begins, "No road offers more mystery than that first one you mount from the town you were born in, the first time you mount it of your own volition, on a trip funded by your own coffee tin of wrinkled-up dollar bills you've saved and scrounged for, worked all-night switchboard for, missed the Rolling Stones for, sold fragrant pot with smashed flowers going brown inside twist-tie plastic baggies for . . ."? You will likely read this 1970s coming-of-age saga seemingly in one breath and then you will go running to read the prequel, *The Liar's Club*, from this brilliant *New York Times* bestselling author.

Memoirs of Childhood and Youth by Albert Schweitzer and C. T. Campion (Syracuse University Press, 1997). A short but powerful classic in which the Nobel laureate shares his remembrances of childhood moments that helped shape one of the most brilliant minds of the last century.

The Woman Warrior: Memoirs of a Girlhood among Ghosts by Maxine Hong Kingston (Vintage, 1989). The dichotomy of Maxine Hong Kingston's world—the America she knows and in which she belongs, and the China that is just as real, even if only experienced through her mother's storytelling and her own desperate imagination. This book is enjoyable in the same way that Amy Tan's fiction embodies the cultural conflicts central to the lives of children of Chinese immigrants, only Kingston's stories are (mostly) true.

Trying to Float: Coming of Age in the Chelsea Hotel by Nicolaia Rips (Scribner, 2016). This memoir is the answer to the question: What would it be like to grow up in a hotel . . . and not just any hotel, but one filled with legends and colorful tenants, not the least of which are the author at seventeen and her parents?

MOTHER MEMOIRS

Are You My Mother?: A Comic Drama by Alison Bechdel (Mariner Books, 2013). Alison Bechtel, the best-selling author of *Fun Home: A Family Tragicomic,* turns her wit and artistic genius to the story of her mother. In her trademark comic-strip prose, Bechtel turns the mundane interactions of a daughter and mother into art of both a visual and literary kind.

Mom & Me & Mom by Maya Angelou (Random House, 2013). Maya Angelou and her mother are like the rain and the wind, each a force of nature in her own right, but together, a hurricane of intention . . . irrepressible.

My Mother Was Nuts: A Memoir by Penny Marshall (New Harvest, 2012). Celebrity memoirs draw us in because we are curious about the genesis of genius and talent. Marshall tries to convince us that she was just an ordinary third child from a colorful family. But it's clear from the beginning that she is "different" even in the early years, and her difference, which is not always so appreciated by her family, is what soon blossoms into something exceptional. Her stories about her mother are hysterical.

With or Without You by Domenica Ruta (Spiegel & Grau, 2013). This coming-of-age, mother-daughter memoir discloses the dizzying complexity of Ruta's mother's twisted morality, utter lawlessness, and unconventional mothering, with wit and clear-eyed frankness. "It's a raw but elegantly told tale, about living with a mother who was an addict and sometime dealer, who loved movies and let her daughter stay home from school when *The Godfather* was on television—and who would take that daughter along on an expedition to bash in the windshield of a woman who'd broken her brother's heart." —NPR

The Long Goodbye: A Memoir by Meghan O'Rourke (Riverhead Books, 2012). O'Rourke chronicles the illness and death of her mother, with whom she was very close.

Moonlight on Linoleum: A Daughter's Memoir by Terry Helwig and Sue Monk Kidd (Howard Books, 2011). The oldest of six girls, Helwig navigates for herself and her sisters a complicated mother; a loving stepfather who is often away, and the frequent relocations of her family from one oil town to another.

So Far Away: A Daughter's Memoir of Life, Loss, and Love by Christine Hartmann (Vanderbilt University Press, 2011). In the difficult place between a well-maintained mother who decides years in advance to end her life at age seventy, and a father who is utterly taken by surprise by his illness (a series of debilitating strokes), Hartmann offers a personal and poignant portrayal of a daughter's dilemma with her parents' end-of-life predicaments.

Lies My Mother Never Told Me by Kaylie Jones (Harper Perennial, 2010). The daughter of James Jones, the award-winning author of *From Here to Eternity,* and Gloria, a charismatic, alcoholic mother. "Searing, brutally honest . . . What makes *Lies My Mother Never Told Me* such an uplifting book despite all the pain and turmoil it recounts is its revelation of how Kaylie Jones has matured as a person in dealing with her twin legacies, literary and alcoholic, and also as a writer." —*Washington Times*

The Color of Water: A Black Man's Tribute to His White Mother by James McBride (Riverhead Trade, 1996). This is a classic must read, so well written and so socially compelling. Biracial McBride tells the story of his Jewish mother, who raises him and his siblings in Harlem, as a single mother.

Love and Relationship Memoirs

Bad Feminist: Essays by Roxane Gay (Harper Perennial, 2014). This collection of essays about the author's life and observations about the world, where and how she fits into it, is hard to categorize for purposes of my list. She pretty much covers all subjects, especially race, gender, and sexuality, with a sharp, astute and hilarious honestly. She is a cultural critic, who uses her own stories to disarm and inform, shock and thrill.

Paris: A Love Story: A Memoir by Kati Marton (Simon & Schuster, 2013). Kati Marton, former foreign correspondent and author, shares an intimate portrayal of the loves of her life (famous men Peter Jennings and Richard Holbrooke) and how the seminal moments of her life, including her romances, found their beginnings and endings in the City of Love and Light.

One Hundred Names for Love: A Stroke, a Marriage, and the Language of Healing by Diane Ackerman (W. W. Norton & Company, 2012). This story is about the endurance of a mature marriage between two writers in the face of a catastrophic stroke. "A gorgeously engrossing, affecting, sweetly funny, and mind-opening love story of crisis, determination, creativity, and repair." —*Booklist*

The New York Regional Mormon Singles Halloween Dance: A Memoir by Elna Baker (Plume, 2010). This delightful memoir about being alone, Mormon, and searching for love in New York City is: "A wickedly funny debut. Baker is both self-absorbed and generous, whip-smart and naive; she apologizes for none of it." —*People*

Let's Take the Long Way Home: A Memoir of Friendship by Gail Caldwell (Random House Trade Paperbacks, 2011). This is the *New York Times* bestseller by award-winning book critic Gail Caldwell about her close and enduring friendship with Caroline Knapp, author of *Drinking: A Love Story*, a friendship that must endure Knapp's cancer diagnosis and treatment.

Burmese Lessons: A True Love Story by Karen Connelly (Nan A. Talese, 2010). Connelly visits Burma to write about political prisoners during a period of the country's political unrest in the late 1990s. While there, she falls in love with a sexy, charismatic leader of a resistance group. "In radiant prose layered with passion, regret, sensuality, and wry humor, *Burmese Lessons* tells the captivating story of how one woman came to love a wounded, beautiful country and a gifted man who has given his life to the struggle for political change." —Penguin Random House

Love, Life, and Elephants: An African Love Story by Dame Daphne Jenkins Sheldrick (Picador, 2013). This is two love stories. One is about how the author falls in love with the reserve, where she helps to save orphan elephants. And the second is the love story between Daphne and the park warden, who shares her passion.

With All My Love, Misty: Memoir of a Broken Heart by Misty DiLello Covington (WiDo Publishing, 2012). The marriage between two unlikely lovers ends on one unfortunate night. And the person who is left behind must piece together what happened in the midst of her grief.

Love Shrinks: A Memoir of a Marriage Counselor's Divorce by Sharyn Wolf (Soho Press, 2011). A paradoxical story by a relationship expert whose professional life blossomed as her own marriage was falling apart.

We Never Lost Hope: A Holocaust Memoir and Love Story by Naomi Litvin and Sir Martin Gilbert (BookSurge Publishing, 2008). "Using the first-person accounts of her parents, an aunt, an uncle, and a friend of the family, the author offers a nuanced and multifaceted look at the plight of Jews in mid-twentieth-century Eastern Europe." —*Kirkus Reviews*

CAREER MEMOIRS

The titles of career memoirs are almost always self-explanatory. Here is an enjoyable selection:

Stir: My Broken Brain and the Meals That Brought Me Home by Jessica Fechtor (Plume, 2016). A gift to foodies, this delightful read is not so much a memoir about food and health. It's about the social-emotional healing of cooking, and feeding the self and loved ones, and how the author used her love for everything culinary to return from a catastrophic brain illness back to her normal self.

Lab Girl by Hope Jahren (Knopf, 2016). Dr. Jahren makes you want to hug a tree, plant a garden, and go back to school to study long and hard enough to be a cool science chick like her. Her memoir is both a professional story and a love story. Her deep affection for the rooted lives that surround us is contagious.

A Natural Woman: A Memoir by Carole King (Grand Central Publishing, 2013). The revealing memoir of one of America's most beloved singer-songwriters. We know the words to her songs, so the stories behind their meanings make for fascinating reading.

The Buy Side: A Wall Street Trader's Tale of Spectacular Excess by Turney Duff (Crown Business, 2013).

Get Well Soon!: My (Un)Brilliant Career as a Nurse by Kristy Chambers (University of Queensland Press, 2013).

Happy, Happy, Happy: My Life and Legacy as the Duck Commander by Phil Robertson and Mark Schlabach (Howard Books, 2013). By the star of the reality show *Duck Dynasty.*

Challenging Beliefs: Memoirs of a Career by Tim Noakes and Michael Vlismas (Random House Struik, 2012). Memoir by well-known exercise physiologist, Tim Noakes.

Heart Matters: A Memoir of a Female Heart Surgeon by Kathy Magliato, MD (Harmony, 2011).

It Worked for Me: In Life and Leadership by Colin Powell with Tony Koltz (HarperCollins Publishers, 2012).

Within Arm's Length: The Extraordinary Life and Career of a Special Agent in the United States Secret Service by Dan Emmett (iUniverse, 2012).

Malled: My Unintentional Career in Retail by Caitlin Kelly (Portfolio, 2011).

Mirthful Memoirs of a Male Nurse by Vince Migliore (CreateSpace, 2010).

My Nine Lives: A Memoir of Many Careers in Music by Leon Fleisher and Anne Midgette (Anchor, 2010).

My Stroke of Insight: A Brain Scientist's Personal Journey by Jill Bolte Taylor, Ph.D. (Plume, 2009).

Model: A Memoir by Cheryl Diamond (Simon Pulse, 2008).

Anna Lee: Memoir of a Career on General Hospital and in Film by Anna Lee and Barbara Roisman Cooper (McFarland, 2007).

Proud Servant: The Memoirs of a Career Ambassador by Ellis Briggs (Kent State University Press, 1998).

TESTIMONY MEMOIRS

Spiritual Misfit: A Memoir of Uneasy Faith by Michelle DeRusha (Convergent Books, 2014). *Library Journal* says of DeRusha, "She writes with unassuming verve and charm reminiscent of Anne Lamott; her frequent admissions of her own shortcomings, doubts, and fears are presented with humor, wit, and intelligence. Her journey and struggle—to accommodate uncertainties within faith—resonate with the experience of many Christians today."

Soil and Sacrament: A Spiritual Memoir of Food and Faith by Fred Bahnson (Simon & Schuster, 2013). This lovely book is fundamentally about how the author found God in gardening and the connection between spiritual and natural life. But it's also about putting faith to work, believing by doing, and how to heal ourselves by healing the Earth.

Wild by Cheryl Strayed (Vintage Books, 2013). Cheryl Strayed, at twenty years old and at her life's rock bottom, decides to hike a thousand miles of the Pacific Crest Trail. Ill-prepared, over-packed, and with unclear purpose, she journeys through one adventure (or misadventure) after another. And though she is often lost, somehow she finds her way and finds herself. A compelling story about what one woman endeavored when she thought she had nothing else to lose.

Sacred Housekeeping: A Spiritual Memoir by Harriet Rossetto (AuthorHouse, 2012). Founder of the renowned Beit T'Shuvah, a nonprofit halfway house for incarcerated Jewish men which evolved into a drug and alcohol treatment facility, Rossetto tells the story with wit and candor of how her unpopular mission came into being. One Amazon reader/reviewer said: "Her stories and connections to Judaism will help anyone who wants to find spirituality or work on their spirituality."

Blackbird Singing in the Dead of Night: What to Do When God Won't Answer by Gregory L. Hunt (Bettie Youngs Books, 2011). Since this memoir offers the reader the opportunity to take a spiritual journey with a pastor—his struggles with faith and private conversations with God—this is a two-fer, both a testimony and a professional journey.

The Dance of the Dissident Daughter: A Woman's Journey from Christian Tradition to the Sacred Feminine by Sue Monk Kidd (HarperOne, 2006). In the middle of an active conventional religious life, Monk Kidd experiences a "feminist spiritual awakening" that is anything but conventional.

Personal Transformation: An Executive's Story of Struggle and Spiritual Awakening by Kiril Sokoloff, Foreword by His Holiness the Dalai Lama (The Crossroad Publishing Company, 2005). Kiril Sokoloff is a successful Wall Street investor and financial advisor, who gradually loses his hearing until becoming entirely deaf. Sokoloff shares his spiritual transformation from loss and loneliness to joy and contentment.

Bibliography

Angelou, Maya, *Mom & Me & Mom.* New York: Random House, 2013.

St. Augustine of Hippo. *Confessions.* Translated and notes by Henry Chadwick. New York: Oxford University Press, 2009.

Currey, Mason. *Daily Ritual: How Artists Work.* New York: Alfred A. Knopf, 2013.

Daniel, Lois. *How to Write Your Own Life Story: The Classic Guide for the Nonprofessional Writer.* Chicago: Chicago Review Press, 1997.

Hagena, Katarina. *The Taste of Apple Seeds.* Translated by Jamie Bulluch. London: Atlantic Books, 2013; originally published in German in 2009.

Hesse, Hermann. *Siddhartha.* Translated by Hilda Rosner. New York: Bantam Classics and New Directions Publishing Corporation, 1981.

Kawasaki, Guy. *Enchantment: The Art of Changing Hearts, Minds, and Actions.* New York: Portfolio, 2012.

Kawasaki, Guy. *The Art of the Start: The Time-Tested, Battle-Hardened Guide for Anyone Starting Anything.* New York: Portfolio, 2004.

Kenyon, Gary M., and William L. Randall. *Restorying Our Lives: Personal Growth through Autobiographical Reflection.* Westport, Connecticut: Praeger Publishers, 1997.

Khoo, Valerie. *Power Stories: The Eight Stories You Must Tell to Build an Epic Business.* Melbourne, Australia: John Wiley & Sons, 2013.

Kidder, Tracy and Richard Todd. *Good Prose: The Art of Nonfiction.* New York: Random House, 2013

King, Stephen. *On Writing: A Memoir of the Craft.* New York: Pocket Books, 2002.

Lamott, Anne. *Bird by Bird: Some Instructions on Writing and Life.* New York: Anchor Books, 1995.

Lee, Kevan. "The Best Time to Write and Get Ideas, According to Science. https://blog.bufferapp.com/the-best-time-to-write-and-get-ideas?utm_source=rss&utm_medium=rss&utm_campaign=the-best-time-to-write-and-get-ideas

Maitland, Sara. *A Book of Silence.* Berkeley: Counterpoint, 2010.

Marton, Kati. *Paris: A Love Story.* New York: Simon & Schuster, 2012.

McClory, Donald. *Introduction to Hermann Hesse.* London: Picador, 1998.

Nepo, Mark. *The Book of Awakening: Having the Life You Want by Being Present to the Life You Have.* San Francisco: Conari Press, 2011.

O'Conner, Patricia T. *Words Fail Me: What Everyone Who Writes Should Know about Writing.* New York: Mariner Books, 2000.

Red Table Talk. https://www.youtube.com/user/RedTable Talks.

Rice, Connie. *Power Concedes Nothing: One Woman's Quest for Social Justice in America, from the Courtroom to the Kill Zones.* New York: Scribner, 2012.

Romance Writers of America. "About the Romance Genre," http://www.rwa.org/p/cm/ld/fid=578.

Smith, Marion Roach, *The Memoir Project: A Thoroughly Non-Standardized Text for Writing and Life.* New York: Grand Central Publishing, 2011.

Strayed, Cheryl. *Wild: From Lost to Found on the Pacific Crest Trail.* New York: Vintage Books, 2013.

Taylor, Daniel, Ph. D. *The Healing Power of Stories: Creating Yourself through the Stories of Your Life.* New York: Doubleday, 1996.

Tóibín, Colm. *New Ways to Kill Your Mother: Writers and Their Families.* New York: Scribner, 2012.

University of Chicago Staff. *Chicago Manual of Style,* Sixteenth *Edition.* Chicago: University of Chicago Press, 2010.

Widrich, Leo. "The Science of Storytelling: Why Telling a Story Is the Most Powerful Way to Activate Our Brains," http://lifehacker.com/5965703/the-science-of-storytelling-why-telling-a-story-is-the-most-powerful-way-to-activate-our-brains, December 5, 2012.

Zinsser, William. *Inventing the Truth: The Art and Craft of Memoir.* New York: Houghton Mifflin Company, 1998.

ACKNOWLEDGMENTS

A book created in solitude is not likely a book worth reading. This one involved the help and generosity of many, and I am deeply thankful for each and every person who touched the manuscript in some way.

I am very grateful to Chicago Review Press for allowing me to share Lois Daniel's concept of ground rules to help us get started. And to the wonderfully insightful authors and teachers who generously share their knowledge through their own books, and whose spot-on insights about how to craft a story helped shape this book—in particular, Marion Roach Smith, William Zinsser, and Steve Zousmer.

Special thanks to my editors, Anita Bunkley, Jamarah Harris, and Wayne Parrish, who were so generous with their talents and their hearts. I deeply appreciate their attention to this book and their kindnesses to me.

I am forever grateful to Deborah Daly for offering her formidable publishing expertise and influence on behalf of her friend, helping me make the proper decisions at every turn.

I couldn't ever possibly express the totality of my gratitude for Carol Chambers Benjamin. Her sage advice and timeless insight make many appearances in these pages. We set out on a shared journey to help others enrich the world with their stories. I am the most grateful beneficiary of her gifts and talents, her optimism, and her clear-eyed honesty. She is a constant source of can-do energy and focus.

I must thank the creative mavericks that are my children—Jonathan, Jillian, Jennifer, Jessica, and Jackson. Our household is a beehive, a boxing ring, an incubator, and the perpetual huddle. It is full of passionately opinionated, strong-willed souls, who are relentlessly truthful. I am indebted to each of them for their willingness to be subject and critic, illumination and motivation for this book and all of my work.

And finally, I have deep appreciation for my mother, Toni Davis, and my husband, Jonathan. They are, much to their chagrin, my favorite subjects. And so I thank them for their long-suffering patience and forbearance, but most of all, for their perfection, from which I find endless inspiration.

ABOUT THE AUTHOR

credit: Pam Francis

GINA CARROLL is on a mission to bring authentic voices to the storytelling universe. As a partner at Inspired Wordsmith, a writing, educational, and authorship services company and cocreator of the *Tell Your Story* Workshops at AStoryThatMatters.com, Gina helps aspiring writers and business professionals get their stories in print. Also the author of *24 Things You Can Do with Social Media to Help Get into College*, she helps students use their social media to share their best stories and show their highest selves online. She began writing, blogging, and speaking after leaving a large corporate law practice to become a stay-at-home mom to raise her five children. She is now nationally recognized for her coverage of the parenting and family landscape, including relationships, digital fluency, parenting adolescents, and the cultural importance of storytelling and memoir.

SELECTED TITLES FROM SPARKPRESS

SparkPress is an independent boutique publisher delivering high-quality, entertaining, and engaging content that enhances readers' lives, with a special focus on female-driven work. Visit us at www.gosparkpress.com

The Natives Are Restless, by Constance Hale. $40, 978-1-943006-06-9. Journalist Constance Hale presents the largely untold story of the dance tradition of hula, using the twin keyholes of Kumu Patrick Makuakane (a Hawaii-born, San Francisco-based hula master), and his 350-person arts organization. In the background, she weaves the poignant story of an ancient people and the resilience of their culture.

The House That Made Me: Writers Reflect on the Places and People That Defined Them, edited by Grant Jarret. $17, 978-1-940716-31-2. In this candid, evocative collection of essays, a diverse group of acclaimed authors reflect on the diverse homes, neighborhoods, and experiences that helped shape them—using Google Earth software to revisit the location in the process.

Gravel on the Side of the Road: True Stories from a Broad Who Has Been There, by Kris Radish. $15, 978-1-940716-43-5. A woman who worries about carrying a .38 special in he rpurse, nearly drowns in a desert canyon, flies into the war in Bosnia, dances with the FBI, and spends time with murderers, has more than a few stories to tell. This daring and revealing adventured by beloved novelist Kris Radish is her first book of autobiographical essays.

Gridley Girls, by Meredith First. $17, 978-1-940716-97-8. From the moment Meg Monahan became a peer counselor in high school, she has been keeping her friend's secrets. Flash forward to adulthood when Meg is a recruiter for the world's hippest, most paranoid high-tech company, and now she is paid to keep secrets. When sudden tragedy strikes just before Meg hosts the wedding of her childhood BFF, the women are forced to face their past—and their secrets—in order to move on to their future.

About SparkPress

SparkPress is an independent, hybrid imprint focused on merging the best of the traditional publishing model with new and innovative strategies. We deliver high-quality, entertaining, and engaging content that enhances readers' lives. We are proud to bring to market a list of *New York Times* best-selling, award-winning, and debut authors who represent a wide array of genres, as well as our established, industry-wide reputation for creative, results-driven success in working with authors. SparkPress, a BookSparks imprint, is a division of SparkPoint Studio LLC.

Learn more at GoSparkPress.com